OUTSIDE THE KINGDOM OF THE LORD THERE IS NO NATION WHICH IS GREATER THAN ANY OTHER.
– Haile Selassie, Emperor of Ethiopia

©2024 CATHERINE FET · NORTH LANDING BOOKS · ALL RIGHTS RESERVED

THE BLACK PHARAOHS
8th century BC

In the 8th century BC, Egypt was ruled by the 'Black Pharaohs.' Who were they? They were native black Africans, kings of the ancient African land of Kush that stretched along the Nile valley south of Egypt, in the region known as *Nubia* (present-day Sudan). Nubia gave birth to some of the earliest civilizations, with the first kingdoms flourishing there as early as the 4th millennium BC. The word *Nubia* likely comes from the Nubian 'nub' – gold. Ancient European sources also call the *Kushites* (the Kush tribes) *Ethiopians* – from the Greek word 'Aithiops,' which is made of two roots – 'dark, sun-tanned' and 'face.' The great Ancient Greek epic poem *The Iliad*, written by Homer around 800 BC, says that the Kushites lived 'at the end of the world.' Their feasts were so famous that even the gods of Olympus visited them! "Zeus himself is at the Ocean's river with the Ethiopians, feasting, he and all the heaven-dwellers," wrote Homer. And in Homer's *Odyssey*, "Poseidon, the earthquake lord, made his return from Ethiopia, where he had visited for a celebration held in his honor."

Greek historian Herodotus (5th century BC) wrote, "Where the South declines toward the setting Sun, lies the country called Ethiopia, the last inhabited land in that direction. There gold is obtained in great plenty, huge elephants abound, with wild trees of all sorts, and ebony…The Ethiopians are said to be the tallest and the most handsome men in the whole world. In their customs they differ greatly from the rest of mankind, and particularly in the way they choose their kings. They find a man who is the tallest of all the citizens, and of strength equal to his height, and appoint him to rule over them…"

Statue of the Kushite King Senkamanisken (640 – 620 BC) reconstruction (The Louvre, Paris, France)

"...Most Ethiopians live to be a hundred and twenty years old, while some even go beyond that age. They eat boiled meat, and drink nothing but milk..." Herodotus also shared this report heard from travelers to Ethiopia: "The Ethiopians were clothed in the skins of leopards and lions, and had long bows made of the stem of the palm-leaf... On these they laid short arrows made of reed, and armed at the tip, not with iron, but with a piece of stone, sharpened to a point. They carried spears, the head of which were the sharpened horns of antelopes, and, in addition, they had knotted clubs. When they went into battle they painted their bodies, half with chalk, and half with vermilion...." (Herodotus, *The Histories*, Book III)

EBONY

Ebony is the wood of a few species of trees growing in Africa and Asia. Ebony wood is black in color and so dense that it sinks in water! Objects made of ebony can be polished to a mirror-like shine. The word 'ebony' comes from the Ancient Egyptian language. Right: Old piano keys made from African ebony and ivory (elephant tusks).

VERMILION

Vermilion is a bright red mineral pigment made until the 19th century from mercury-rich ore called 'cinnabar.' A cinnabar crystal.

The Kushite city-state of Kerma, or Kush, emerged in the 3rd millennium BC. For one thousand years Kush controlled the Nile Valley from the 1st cataract of the Nile to the spot where the **Blue Nile** and the **White Nile** merge (present-day Khartoum in Sudan). Kush had gold mines in the desert near its capital city of Napata. It produced bronze tools and traded goods up and down the Nile, selling ebony, ostrich feathers, leopard skins, and the precious oils used in perfume-making. In the 2nd millennium BC, Kush was conquered by Egypt and ruled by the Egyptians for 500 years.

The sandals of King Tut (Pharaoh Tutankhamun, 14th century BC) had images of Syrian and Nubian prisoners on the soles, so that the king could trample these enemies of Egypt under his feet every day. But, following the **Late Bronze Age Collapse** Egypt grew weaker, and in the 700s BC King Kashta ("the Kushite") took over Thebes and became King of **Upper Egypt**.

The Late Bronze Age Collapse – 12th Century BC

The Late Bronze Age Collapse was a catastrophic destruction and decline of many Mediterranean civilizations during the transition from the **Bronze Age** to the **Iron Age**. It may have been caused by the mass migration of the so-called **Sea Peoples** – tribes from the east of the Mediterranean region – toward the west. New methods of warfare and he availability of iron (which is more abundant in nature than the **tin** and **copper** needed to produce **bronze**) made wars more destructive. These wars disrupted trade and caused economic collapse.

Upper and Lower Egypt, Cataracts of the Nile, the Blue Nile and the White Nile

The names **Upper Egypt** and **Lower Egypt** refer to the direction of the flow of the Nile. Since the Nile flows from South to North, Upper Egypt is 'higher' up the river, 'upstream' (in the South), while Lower Egypt is 'down the river' closer to the **Delta** of the Nile (in the North).

The **Cataracts** of the Nile are whitewater rapids – fast-flowing and turbulent stretches of the river – on the Nile between Khartoum (Sudan) and Aswan (Egypt). There are 6 cataracts of the Nile.

The **Blue Nile** and the **White Nile** are **tributaries** (smaller rivers flowing into a larger river) of the Nile River. The Blue Nile originates in Lake Tana in Ethiopia. The White Nile flows from Lake Victoria, the largest lake in Africa, which is divided between Tanzania, Uganda, and Kenya. The Blue and the White join in Khartoum, the capital of Sudan and flow to Egypt. The Blue Nile is not blue at all! It's dark because of the red-brown clay in its river bed. But in Sudanese Arabic the word 'azraq' (الأزرق) means both blue and black. So maybe it's the 'Black Nile'? The White Nile is named after the white clay in its river bed that gives its waters a whitish tint.

The First Cataract of the Nile

Kashta's takeover of Thebes was peaceful. Realizing that in order to rule Egypt, Nubians would have to adopt Egyptian culture, religion, and rituals, Kashta made sure his daughter was selected as the next High Priestess – or "God's Wife" of the god Amun in Thebes. This worked. Even the grandkids of the previous pharaoh accepted his rule. Despite his success, Kashta himself preferred to live at a safe distance from Thebes. He ruled Upper Egypt from the city of Napata in modern-day Sudan. Unlike most Egyptian pharaohs, Kashta seems to have had only one wife. They had 5 or 6 kids. Kashta's son, Piye became the first "Black Pharaoh" to rule both Upper and Lower Egypt (744–714 BC). He restored the Great Temple of Amun built by Egyptian Pharaoh Thutmose III in the 13th century BC and – just like his dad – made one of his daughters the High Priestess of Amun. Piye had four wives and over 10 kids.

After 20 years on the throne of Upper Egypt, Piye grew very powerful. The princes and warlords of Lower Egypt knew that sooner or later the Nubians would invade Lower Egypt. To prevent this, they bribed Nimlot, one of Piye's allies, to join forces with them. Under the command of a Libyan chieftain, Tefnakhte, they besieged the Nubian garrison in the town of Herakleopolis ("City of Heracles" in Greek). This conspiracy against Piye turned out to be a big mistake. In no time Piye raised a powerful army and invaded Lower Egypt. He proclaimed his campaign a 'holy war' against the enemies of Amun, and ordered all his soldiers to perform purification rituals before going into battle.

Below: Head of a Kushite ruler (8th century BC); Head of Chepenoupet II, daughter of King Piye, wearing the crown of the goddess Hathor. Right: Piye's Stela (reconstruction).

The text on the granite *stela* (stela/stele = a stone slab/pillar with an inscription) of Piye describing his victory reads: "His Majesty sent word to the lords and generals who were in Egypt, 'Proceed in battle formation, engage in combat, encircle and defeat them. Capture their people, herds, and ships on the river. Do not allow the farmers to go into the fields! Do not allow the plowmen to plow!...When you arrive in Thebes, enter into the water and purify yourselves in the river. Clothe yourselves in the best linen. Lay down the bow, withdraw the arrow. Do not brag about how strong you are, because Amun makes even the broken-armed strong... Sprinkle yourselves with the water of his altars. You should kiss the ground before him and you should say to him: Give us passage, that we might fight in the shadow of your strong arm!'"

Piye's army defeated the Libyan river fleet on the Nile, and took Herakleopolis, plus Nimlot's princedom of Hermopolis, and Memphis, Egypt's ancient capital! The Lower Egypt warlords surrendered. Their leader Tefnakhte escaped to an island in the Nile Delta and sent Piye a letter recognizing his defeat and describing his humiliation as vividly as possible, hoping for mercy. "Peace be with you!" says the letter as quoted on a stela that recorded the events of Piye's reign. "I cannot look upon your face – of shame. I cannot stand before you, for I am terrified of your fiery greatness. Bitterness is in my bones, my head is balding, my clothes are rags!... Take my property for your treasury – gold and every sort of gemstone, and the best of my horses, and any payment you wish to receive from me. Send me a messenger so that he can calm down my fear... Then I shall go to the temple in his presence to cleanse myself by a divine oath." The oath read, "I shall not transgress the royal command. I shall not ignore what His Majesty Piye says. I shall act in accordance with what the king has said." Piye didn't care for revenge. Once Tefnakhte swore this oath of loyalty, Piye left him alone.

Nimlot also begged for forgiveness and sent Piye gifts of "silver, gold, lapis lazuli, turquoise, copper, and every sort of gemstone in great quantity" to save his life. He also gave Piye a horse and a sistrum – a rattle-like musical instrument. "His Majesty then proceeded to the house of King Nimlot," narrates the Piye Stela, "and he went into every room in his palace, into the treasury and his storehouses. He ordered that the royal wives and the royal daughters be presented to him. They came and greeted His Majesty with feminine flirtation, but His Majesty did not pay attention to them and proceeded to the stable... When he saw the horses, he realized they were thin and hungry, and he said: "As I live, as god Amun loves me, how much more pain I feel in my heart that these horses have been starved than over any other crime you have committed!" So Nimlot's property was seized and given to the temple of Amun in Karnak.

Nubians considered the Nile Delta inhabitants 'impure' because they ate fish. For that reason the Piye Stela portrays Nimlot standing, while the 'impure' Delta warlords – kneeling. Piye was quite happy with this outcome of the war and couldn't wait to leave for Nubia. So he took a boat up the Nile and never again returned to Egypt.

The Nubian 'Black Pharaohs' ruled Egypt for about a hundred years. During their reign, the Kushites not only adopted the worship of Egyptian gods, but also started mummifying their dead, and building their own pyramids. There are ruins of over 200 pyramids in the area of the ancient Kushite capital of *Meroe* (present-day Sudan). That's more pyramids than in all of Egypt!

In the 600s BC, the Nubians were driven out of Egypt by the Assyrians. The Assyrians had iron tools and weapons, while the Nubians were still a Bronze-Age culture. Soon, however, it was discovered that the lands of Kush were rich in iron ore, so the Kushites began iron production. This supported their kingdom for another 1,000 years! During this era, the Kingdom of Kush was conquered by Egypt, and then by the Greeks, and then by the Romans. But what eventually destroyed Kush was an environmental disaster. Iron production requires large quantities of charcoal. The Kushites cut down the trees faster than the trees could regrow. This caused soil erosion, a decline of agriculture, and horrific famines. The population of Kush shrank and by AD 350 Kush had been destroyed by the Kingdom of Aksum (present-day Northern Ethiopia).

Almost everything we know about the Kingdom of Kush comes from Egyptian sources. The native language of the Kushites – *Meroitic* – has still never been deciphered! 'Meroitic' comes from Meroe. Defeated by the Assyrians, the Kushites moved their capital from Napata further South, to Meroe.

Meroe pyramids and Meroitic writing

The Iron Age in Africa

Ironworking likely originated in a few areas of the ancient world between 1500-1000 BC. One place where this happened was modern-day Turkey. Another was Central Africa - present-day Chad, Sudan, South Sudan and the Central African Republic. Iron smelting was probably discovered while firing ceramics. Archaeological evidence shows that iron smelting existed in sub-Saharan Africa centuries before it was introduced in Egypt.

Queen Amanirenas
1st century BC

Nubian Queen Amanirenas ruled the Kingdom of Kush from around 40 BC. On a Meroitic-language stella recording the events of her reign, her name appears along with two male names – most likely her son and her husband. As Amanirenas started her reign in Kush, Egypt was ruled by the famous Cleopatra. Unlike Amanirenas, who was a native African, Cleopatra was Greek – a descendant of Ptolemy Soter, one of the generals of Alexander the Great. In the 1st century, Rome emerged as the Mediterranean superpower, and Egypt became a target for Roman conquest. Gold-rich Kush was also a potential target, but it was distant and unexplored by the Romans, while Egypt had absorbed so much Greek and Roman culture over the 3 centuries of the *Hellenistic Era*, that Romans felt at home there.

Hellenistic Era

*The term **Hellenistic** comes from the Ancient Greek name for Greece – **Hellas** (Ἑλλάς). The Hellenistic Era is a period of European history between the conquests of Alexander the Great (336 – 323 BC) and the conquest of Egypt by Rome (and the death of Cleopatra) in 30 BC. During this era Greek culture dominated the Mediterranean.*

To preserve Egypt's independence, Cleopatra bet everything on her personal ties to Roman politicians. First she had a relationship (and a couple kids!) with the Roman dictator Julius Caesar. After Caesar was assassinated by conspirators, his general and ally, Mark Antony, moved to Egypt to live with Cleopatra. But Cleopatra's strategy backfired. A conflict between Antony and Octavian, Caesar's nephew and heir, resulted in war. In 31 BC a Roman fleet led by Octavian defeated the Egyptians in the famous naval battle at Actium. Egypt fell. Cleopatra and Antony committed suicide.

Left: Cleopatra; Below: Meroe

In the south, in the Kingdom of Kush, these events caused a lot of concern. Queen Amanirenas believed Kush was next on the list to be invaded by Rome. Amanirenas' contemporary, Greek geographer and historian Strabo, who traveled to both Egypt and Kush and knew that region well, referred to Amanirenas as Κανδάκη – Kandake, often translated as 'Candace.' Actually, 'Kandake' was the title of the Nubian queen, not her name. Strabo describes Amanirenas as "a masculine woman, blind in one eye." Rather than waiting for the Roman invasion, Queen Amanirenas decided to surprise the Romans with an attack by the Kushite forces. According to Strabo's book *Geography*, the Kushite army marched against three Egyptian cities controlled by the Romans – Syene (Aswan), Elephantina, and Philae – and captured them. "The Ethiopians invaded the Thebaid and attacked the garrison, consisting of three cohorts, near Syene. With a surprise attack they took Syene, Elephantina, and Philæ, enslaved their inhabitants, and knocked down the statues of Caesar." 'Caesar' in this passage is Octavian, who was proclaimed Roman Emperor Octavian Augustus in 27 BC. Indeed, in 1913, a British archaeologist discovered a bronze head from a statue of Octavian Augustus – nicknamed the 'Meroe head.' It was buried under the staircase of an ancient temple dedicated to the Greek goddess Nike – Victory – in the Kushite capital Meroe.

Romans were not intimidated by Queen Amanirenas' troops. Octavian appointed a new **prefect** (governor) of Egypt, Gaius Petronius, who led 10 thousand Roman infantrymen and 800 horsemen against the 30-thousand-strong army of Queen Amanirenas. Romans were much better armed than the Nubians. Their military skill and tactics were legendary. Nubians "had bad commanders and were badly armed," wrote Strabo. "They carried large shields made of raw hides, and hatchets for offensive weapons. Some had pikes, and others swords." The Nubians were pushed back. Petronius sent messengers to the Nubian commanders asking to return the statues and treasures from the cities they had captured and looted. He also inquired about "the reasons which had caused them to begin the war." The Nubians stated that they were fighting Egyptian warlords serving the Romans. "These are nobodies, the only ruler is Caesar," said Petronius and gave the Nubians three days to return the loot. The Nubians, however, ignored the Romans' demands. So, the Romans pushed forward into the Kingdom of Kush, taking town after town. Finally, the Romans approached the city of Napata.

"This was the royal seat of Candace, and her son was there, but she herself was in a neighboring stronghold," wrote Strabo. "She sent ambassadors to the Romans asking for peace, and offered to return the prisoners and the statues, but Petronius attacked and took Napata, from which her son had fled, and razed the city to the ground." Then Petronius returned to Egypt, "as he judged any further advance impractical because of bad roads." He sold Nubian prisoners into slavery, "a thousand were sent to Caesar, others died of various diseases."

But that wasn't the end of the war. Once Petronius left, Amanirenas' "army of many thousand men" attacked the city of Premnis guarded by a Roman garrison. Petronius rushed back and was met on the ruins of the city by Nubian ambassadors sent by Queen Amanirenas. This time around he had much more respect for his enemy, so he suggested the Nubians should negotiate with Caesar (Octavian Augustus) himself. The ambassadors replied they "did not know who Caesar was, nor where to find him." Then Petronius arranged for the Nubians to travel to the Greek island of Samos, where Octavian stayed on his way to Syria. Nubians were good diplomats. "The ambassadors received everything they desired," reports Strabo. "Caesar even forgave them the *tribute* they were supposed to pay." Peace between Rome and the Kingdom of Kush lasted for 300 years – until Kush was conquered and destroyed by its rival, the Kingdom of Aksum. Nubians traded with Romans throughout that peaceful era, selling mostly ivory and slaves – prisoners of tribal wars. Queen Amanirenas became a legendary heroine, one of few native rulers who stood up to the Romans, never gave up the sovereignty of her state, never paid tribute to the Roman empire, never *ceded* an inch of land.

tribute – *a payment imposed by a stronger state on a weaker state as a sign of domination or as a punishment for waging a war*
to cede – *to give up power or territory*

Meroe pottery (1st century AD); Meroe pyramids

Ezana of Axum
300s – 360 AD

King Ezana of Axum ruled the giant Kingdom of Aksum – present-day Ethiopia, Eritrea, Yemen, and Sudan – from its capital Axum, for about 40 years, starting in the 320s. King Ezana was one of the first rulers in the world to make Christianity the state religion. He is regarded as a saint by both the Catholic Church and the Ethiopian Orthodox Church.

Aksum's inhabitants were native tribes of North Africa and Arabia. They spoke *Ge'ez* and *Sabaean* – South Arabian **Semitic languages** related to modern Amharic (Ethiopian), Arabic, and Hebrew. By the 2nd century the Kingdom of Aksum dominated trade around the Red Sea. Its ships carried gold and ivory to Rome and India. Aksum minted its own coins and built massive temples and monuments. Some of its stone obelisks were over 100 feet (30 meters) tall.

When Ezana's dad died and he inherited the throne of the Kingdom of Aksum, Ezana was still a kid. His mother, Queen Sofya, turned to two men she trusted. Both were Syrian slaves freed by her husband, King Ella Amida. Tyrannius Rufinus, a 4th-century Roman Christian historian tells their story. Two Syrian boys from Christian families – Frumentius and Aedesius – happened to be on a ship attacked by pirates. They were captured and sold into slavery to the Kingdom of Aksum and ended up at the court of Ezana's dad. King Ella Amida gave his slaves Frumentius and Aedesius an excellent education, and when they grew up he granted them freedom, and appointed them royal government officials. Queen Sofya asked them to help her raise young Ezana, and Frumentius became his teacher. Frumentius also helped the Queen in governing her territory, and used his position of power to help Christian traders.

Above: King Ezana's coin;
Below: Ezana's obelisk in Axum
(a 19th-century print)

After Ezana grew up and became king, Frumentius traveled to Egypt. In Alexandria, he asked the leaders of the Eastern Orthodox Christian Church to send a bishop to the Kingdom of Aksum. They suggested that Frumentius become that bishop himself. They ordained him a priest, and by the time he reached Aksum he was a bishop! Under his influence Ezana converted to Christianity. The early stone pillar inscriptions of his reign give him the title 'the Son of Ares' (Greek god of war), but on the coins from his later years the pagan symbols of the Sun disk and the Moon crescent are replaced with the Christian cross. Ezana led the troops of Aksum in a number of military campaigns. The most famous of these was the conquest and destruction of the Kingdom of Kush and its capital, Meroe, in AD 330. Ezana's reign was the peak of Aksum's prosperity. Some Aksum coins he minted bear the inscription "May this please the country" in Greek, which indicates that King Ezana cared deeply about trade and about the well-being of his people.

The name of King Ezana will also be found in Ethiopian legends about the *Ark of the Covenant*. According to the Old Testament of the Bible, the Ark was a wooden chest covered with gold. It was built to carry the stone *Tablets of the Law* with the *Ten Commandments* inscribed on them. The tablets were given by God to Moses. Once King Solomon of Israel (10 - 9th centuries BC) built the *Jerusalem Temple*, the Ark was kept in the Temple's inner sanctuary, the *Holy of Holies*. In 587 BC the Babylonians conquered Jerusalem and destroyed the Temple, but, even though the Bible mentions the treasures they took from the Temple, the Ark is not mentioned. And at this point it completely disappears from the biblical narrative. Was it destroyed? Was it hidden? According to Ethiopian legends the Ark was gone from the Jerusalem Temple centuries before the Babylonian Invasion. It was stolen by Menelik, the son of King Solomon and Queen Sheba of the Kingdom of Saba (present-day Yemen and Ethiopia). Menelik brought the Ark to the Kingdom of Aksum, and, centuries later, King Ezana moved it to his capital, Axum, and placed it in the treasury of the church he built there – the Church of Our Lady Mary of Zion. The Ethiopian Orthodox Church claims that the Ark is, indeed, in its possession. Only one person is allowed to see it – a guardian chosen from local monks. The legends hint at the magic powers of the Ark that affect its guardians' vision – over the span of their lives they all turn blind!

"The Ark of Covenant" by James Tissot

Sundiata Keita
1217 – 1255

The Empire of Mali was founded in the 1200s by an African ruler named Sundiata Keita, often called the "Lion King." The empire stretched across West African lands of the Mandinka people which today belong to Mali, Senegal, Gambia, Guinea, Niger, Nigeria, Chad, Mauritania, and Burkina Faso. The Mali Empire lasted through the 16th century. Sundiata Keita's life became the focus of legends that were gathered into a collection called the *Epic of Sundiata*. The poems that make up the epic were recited by traveling singers called 'griots.' We also learn about Sundiata Keita's reign from Moroccan and Tunisian travelers who visited the Mali Empire in the 14th century.

According to the *Epic of Sundiata*, Sundiata Keita was a son of the Mandinka king of the Kangaba state which was part of the Ghana Empire of West Africa. He was crippled from birth and unable to walk. The king had many wives and kids, and all of them made fun of Sundiata's disability and his mom's sadness. This forced Sundiata to fight for his future, and after years of attempts, one day he stood up, started walking, and soon was recognized as a leader among the royal kids. This caused a lot of envy, and when Sundiata's dad died, his relatives chased Sundiata and his mom into exile. The king of Mema, a small kingdom in Mali, allowed them to stay at his court. He admired Sundiata's courage, and made him his top government official. But Sundiata's destiny was to return to his native land.

The Great Mosque in Djenne, Mali

The King of Sosso (present-day Ghana) conquered the Mandinka lands. Defeated Mandinka war lords looked for any glimpse of hope, and learned of a prophecy saying that only one man could liberate their homeland – Sundiata. They begged Sundiata to return, and he came back with a well-trained army given to him by the king of Mema. Sundiata and the Mandinka chiefs won the Battle of Kirina on the Niger River, and Sundiata became the first **Mansa** ('emperor' in the Mandinka language) of the Mali Empire.

One of the Arab travelers to Mali recorded the story of the Battle of Kirina as he had heard it recited among the Mandinka: "They met in a place called Kirina. When Sundiata saw the army of Sumanguru, the King of Sosso, he asked, 'Isn't there a cloud over there in the East?' But they told him it was the army of Sumanguru. And Sumanguru exclaimed: 'What is that mountain of stone over there in the West?' And they told him: 'It is the army of Sundiata.' Then the two armies came together and fought a battle. In the middle of the fight, Sundiata uttered a great shout, and all the warriors of Sumanguru fled and hid behind Sumanguru. Then Sumanguru uttered a great shout, and all the warriors of Sundiata fled to hide behind Sundiata... Then Sundiata said, 'Have you forgotten the great prophecy?' He was talking about the prophecy of Sumanguru's death. Then one of his soldiers came forward with an arrow that had a spur of a white rooster as an arrowhead. He shot the arrow at Sumanguru, saying 'This is the arrow of the man who knows the ancient secrets.' As soon as it struck Sumanguru, he vanished and was seen no more. Sumanguru had a gold bracelet on his wrist. It fell on that spot, and a baobab tree grew out of it and it's there to this day."

Timbuktu (19th-century print)

In Koulikoro, Mali — a sign marking the spot where Sumanguru vanished: "Nianankulu: Sumanguru disappeared here in 1235" (in French)

Generation on generation of the Mandinka people have preserved the **Manden Charter** (also known as the **Kouroukan Fouga**) – one of the world's earliest codes of human rights. The charter was not a written document, but a collection of 44 *edicts* or unwritten laws created by Sundiata after the Battle of Kirina and passed down as an oral tradition. It describes the Empire of Mali as a federation of Mandinka clans ruled by Sundiata's royal family.

Here is a summary of the most remarkable among the Charter's unwritten laws:

- Everyone has the right to live. Murder is punished with death.
- To achieve prosperity, the leaders of the clans will fight against laziness and idleness among their people.
- The *sanankuya* or 'joking relationship' should be adopted between clans and individual clan members to preserve peace and learn tolerance. The 'joking relationship' is a form of friendly 'roasting' – a West African social tradition where fellow tribesmen or family members exchange permissions to poke fun at each other, or even organize a contest of humorous 'insults' held in front of an audience. This tradition is alive in West Africa. For instance, members of the Traoré and Koné clans in Mali and Burkina Faso still today compete in accusing each other of being addicted to eating beans!
- The education of the children is the duty of every member of the society.
- Never offend women.
- If a statement suspected to be a lie has not been disproven for 40 years, it should be considered truth.
- Vanity is a sign of weakness. Humility is a sign of greatness.
- Never betray one another. Respect your Word of Honor.
- Do not mistreat foreigners.

Above: Djinguereber Mosque, Mali, and Kurukanfuga Kaaba, the place where Mandinka people gathered in 1236 to adopt the Manden Charter as the law of their land.

- Any object lost and not claimed by an owner for 4 years, becomes the property of the clan.
- To take and eat food that doesn't belong to you is not theft as long as you eat it where you found it and don't take it away.
- You can kill the enemy, but do not humiliate him.
- Do not mistreat the slaves. Give them one day off each week and let them finish their daily work at a reasonable time. You are the master of the slaves, not a burden they should be forced to carry.

Trans-Saharan Slave Trade

After the death of the Prophet Muhammad in 632, Muslim Arabs sought to spread Islam in the Mediterranean and North Africa. Soon most of North Africa embraced Islam. So did some kingdoms of West and East Africa, including Mali. This was the time of the Dark Ages in Europe when rapid population growth made slavery unnecessary. In the Islamic world, however – from Arabia to Morocco and Islamic Spain – they were still dependent on slave labor.

Enslaving Muslims or non-Muslim residents of Islamic states was prohibited by Islamic law. However, purchasing slaves from non-Muslim societies was not only permitted, but also encouraged. And so it was that the ancient trans-Saharan slave routes – unused since the decline of the Roman Empire – were revived at the end of the 7th century.

In African societies slavery was widespread and commonly accepted. The countries of the Sahel became the main suppliers of African slaves. Their customers were Muslim slave traders. From the 7th to the 16th century about 6 million Africans were brought to the slave markets of North Africa by the Trans-Saharan routes. In the 17th and 18th centuries, 1.2 million slaves were delivered. Untold numbers of captured Africans died crossing the Sahara Desert. The first Muslim country to make slavery illegal was Tunisia – in 1846. The last was Mauritania – in 1981.

The Sahel

The Sahel is a geographical zone in Africa – the dry grasslands located between the Sahara Desert and the savannas to the south of it. The Sahel stretches from the Atlantic Ocean to the Red Sea. It is an extremely dry region, often called the 'Acacia savanna,' since acacia is the most widespread of the few trees that survive in the dry heat. The kingdoms of the Sahel – such as the Ghana, Mali and Songhai empires – grew rich through controlling the trade routes between the Mediterranean Sea and Sub-Saharan Africa (south of the Sahara Desert). Their economic and military power depended on horses and camels. For that reason the great empires of the Sahel never reached the forest zone of Africa, where large caravans and cavalry couldn't pass.

Below: The Sahel
Right: A ceramic sculpture, Mali, 13th century

Mansa Musa
1280 – 1337

Mansa Musa was a great nephew of Sundiata Keita. In the 13th and 14th centuries, when he ruled the Mali Empire, the mines he controlled produced 50% of all the gold and salt – in the world! The wealth of the Mali empire was spectacular, and Musa is still often referred to as the richest man of all time. In that era Europe and the Middle East were torn apart by wars, and ravaged with famines. On that background the legend of Mansa Musa and his wealth grew larger-than-life. The Mali empire's official religion was Islam, and its biggest cities, Djenne and Timbuktu, were prominent centers of Islamic learning and culture. Timbuktu's Sankore University – the oldest university in Sub-Saharan Africa – taught mathematics, law, history, geography, astronomy, and astrology. Its library counted 700,000 manuscripts from around the world. Literacy was considered a sign of 'baraka' – blessing from God. Owning books was so prestigious that the wealthy families boasted more of the books they purchased, than of other riches in their possession.

As Musa was growing up, the *mansa* (king) of the Mali Empire was his cousin, Muhammad, a grandson of Sundiata Keita. However, Muhammad wasn't happy just being king. He dreamed of adventures. One day he equipped hundreds of ships and led an expedition looking for the 'end of the world' or the 'other edge' of the Atlantic ocean. He never returned from this voyage, and in 1307 Musa, in his early 20s, became king. This story was recorded as told by Mansa Musa himself, and scholars suspect perhaps he just overthrew his cousin and made it look like Muhammad was lost at sea.

Mansa Musa as portrayed in the Catalan Atlas (14th century). The caption next to his image reads: "This black Lord is called Mansa Musa and is the sovereign of the land of the black people of Ghana. This king is the richest and noblest due to the abundance of gold that is extracted in his lands."

Through diplomacy and conquest Musa expanded his empire, grew its wealth, and built schools, universities, libraries, and mosques in every town.

In 1324 Mansa Musa became a celebrity across the Muslim world and also in Europe! How did this happen? Musa was a devout Muslim, and in 1324 he decided to go on the **Hajj**. The distance from Timbuktu to Mecca is about 4,000 miles, so Musa brought with him a gigantic caravan of 80 camels, plus horses and elephants carrying royal baggage, thousands of pounds of gold, and gifts for kings and warlords Musa expected to meet on his way to Mecca. The caravan was accompanied by 60 thousand soldiers and 12 thousand slaves and heralds. 500 of them were dressed in embroidered clothes of precious Persian silk and marched in front of Musa's carriage with staffs of pure gold, each weighing 62 ounces (1.8kg)!!!

The Hajj to Mecca

*In Islam, the Hajj is a traditional Muslim **pilgrimage** (a journey to a holy site) to the city of Mecca, in present-day Saudi Arabia. All adult Muslims – men and women – are required to make the Hajj at least once in their lifetime – but only if they can afford to travel and if their absence wouldn't cause problems for their family. Having gone on the Hajj, a Muslim may add the honorary title Hajji / Hajjah (masculine/feminine) to his or her name.*

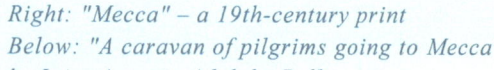

Right: "Mecca" – a 19th-century print
Below: "A caravan of pilgrims going to Mecca" by Leon Auguste Adolphe Belly

When Musa's caravan stopped in Egypt, Mansa Musa gave away so much gold in Cairo that its value plummeted on Egyptian markets and didn't rise again for 12 years! The **Mamluk** Sultan of Cairo, Al-Malik al-Nasir, was eager to meet Musa, but Musa declined because the custom required that he kiss Al-Malik al-Nasir's hand and the ground in front of him. Arab writer Ibn Fadl Allah al Omari, who traveled to Cairo 12 years after Musa's visit, quoted a Cairo official who had met Musa. According to him Musa communicated with Egyptians only through an interpreter, even though he spoke perfect Arabic. "When I went out to greet him in the name of the glorious Sultan Al-Malik al-Nasir, he gave me the warmest of welcomes and treated me with the most careful politeness... I suggested that he should go up to the palace and meet the Sultan. But he refused, saying: 'I came for the pilgrimage, and for nothing else...' However, I well understood that he rejected the meeting because he didn't want to kiss the ground before the Sultan or to kiss his hand. I went on insisting and he went on making excuses. But court rules obliged me to present him to the sultan, and I did not leave him until he had agreed...

...When he came into the Sultan's presence we asked him to kiss the ground. But he refused and continued to refuse, saying: 'Why is this necessary?' Then a wise man of his advisors whispered several words to him that I could not understand. 'Very well,' he said, 'I will prostrate myself, but only before God who created me and brought me into the world.' Having done so he moved towards the Sultan. The Sultan rose for a moment to welcome him and asked him to sit beside him. Then they had a long conversation. After Mansa Musa left the palace the Sultan of Cairo sent him gifts of clothing, and saddled and bridled horses for him and his chief officers."

View of Cairo and a Cairo bazaar – 19th-century prints

Mamluk

The word **Mamluk** comes from the Arabic word for 'slave.' The Mamluks were slaves trained as warriors who served in the armies of Arab and Turkish rulers across the Muslim Middle East and North Africa from the 9th to 16th centuries. Most of the Mamluk slaves came from Turkey and the Northern Caucasus (present-day Russia). Eventually Mamluk military commanders took over some of the lands where their armies operated and established royal dynasties. In the 13th century, Mamluk sultans of Egypt and Syria defeated European crusaders and Mongolian invaders, driving them out of the Middle East.

"A Mamluk fighter" by Emile Jean Horace Vernet

While in Cairo, Musa was equally generous to the ruling class and common people. Visiting the bazaars, he purchased any goods offered to him – most of which he didn't need – paying in gold. Wherever he stopped on a Friday, he built a mosque.

Muhammad ibn Abdullah ibn Battuta, a famous Berber Muslim traveler and writer from Morocco, visited the Empire of Mali in 1352, a few years after Mansa Musa's death. He was impressed with how safe he felt in Mali: "Among the admirable qualities of these people, the following are to be noted: 1. The small number of acts of injustice that one finds there, because the blacks, of all peoples, hate injustice most. Their sultan pardons no one who is guilty of it. 2. The complete safety one enjoys throughout their land. The traveler has no more reason to fear criminals and thieves than the man who stays at home. 3. The blacks do not confiscate the goods of white men who die in their country, not even when these consist of big treasures. They deposit them with trusted people among the whites until the heirs come and take possession of the goods." The "white men" here refers to North Africans – Arabs, Berbers, or Tuaregs – to whom Sub-Saharan Africans referred as 'tribes of the white race.'

Berbers and Tuaregs

Berbers are an ethnic group indigenous to North Africa who populated the present-day territories of Morocco, Algeria, and Libya before the Arabs migrated there from the Middle East as part of the Islamic conquests, starting in the 7th century. Today, Berbers are ethnic minorities living mostly in Morocco and Algeria. Tuaregs are Berber tribes living in the Sahara desert. In the past Tuaregs were **nomadic** (not settled, moving from place to place) goat and camel herders. They controlled many trade routes across the Sahara. A **Tuareg cross** – an amulet traditionally worn by the Tuaregs.

Askia The Great
1443 – 1538

In the 15th century, the Mali Empire declined. In its place rose the Songhai Empire, the biggest ever kingdom in West Africa. Askia Muhammad, a warlord from the city of Gao, Mali, seized the Songhai throne and ruled it between 1492 and 1528 as Askia the Great. Thanks to his conquests, during his reign the Songhai Empire was larger than Western Europe, covering a territory that today is divided between a dozen African states.

Askia Muhammad was born Mohammed Abu Bekr on an island in the Niger River, not far from Timbuktu. When he grew up he joined the army and eventually became one of the top commanders, and also the prime minister of Songhai King Sonni Ali. Sonni Ali had grown his kingdom from a small state in the upper Niger valley into a powerful empire. One of the greatest military leaders in African history, he was also known for his bad temper. He often flew into a rage and made disastrous decisions which he later regretted. Mohammed Abu Bekr was the only man at Sonni Ali's court who wasn't afraid of the king and could stop him during his fits of anger. When Sonni Ali captured Timbuktu, Mali's most important city, he ordered its total destruction. It was Mohammed who prevented the Songhai troops from burning the ancient city. When blinded by rage, the king often ordered one or another of his generals or ministers executed. Mohammed used to hide them in a safe place until the king's rage passed.

People wondered about Mohammed's fearlessness before Sonni Ali. Some were convinced that Mohammed was a child of the king's sister, and that Mohammed's father was a 'jinni,' a magical being from Arabic folk tales.

Warriors in the Sahel, 19th-century print

Sonni Ali and Mohammed would argue for days on end. To help her son, Mohammed's mother secretly spread word of these arguments in the mosques of Timbuktu, asking everyone to pray for Mohammed's success. As a result, many among Sonni Ali's subjects regarded Mohammed Abu Bekr as a wiser and better ruler than the wild and arrogant Sonni Ali.

In 1492, on his way home from a successful military campaign, Sonni Ali drowned when crossing a river. His son Sonni Baru was to be crowned king, but there was a problem. He was loyal to the native religion of his mother's tribe and refused to convert to Islam. This led to a revolt in the army. Mohammed Abu Bekr used this opportunity to unite the Songhai army commanders around himself and defeated Sonni Baru and his brothers. A legend says that when Sonni Ali's daughters heard the news that Mohammed had seized the throne, they shouted, "A si kiya!" which literally means, 'It's not his!' To mock them, Mohammed made 'Askia' his royal title and the name of his dynasty.

Askia the Great grew his empire by conquest, but it was his talent as a civil administrator, a manager, that made it wealthy and powerful. He divided his kingdom into provinces, each ruled by a talented and trusted governor. Askia created positions of 'ministers' who managed finance, courts, agriculture, and so on. All the top jobs were given to his family members. The 'white races' – the **Moors** in the North – were forced to pay tribute to the Songhai crown. The full-time army was replaced with temporary military service allowing more people to work in industry and agriculture. Islam was made the state religion of the empire. Askia supported scholars and hired them as advisors. He built harbors and canals, developed trade along the Niger River and had weights and measures used in the markets standardized and inspected. Universities he funded taught hundreds of students, arts flourished, and chess became the most popular pastime!

*13th-century **madrasa** (religious school) in Timbuktu*

Who were the Moors?

The word **Moor** was used by Christian Europeans to refer to the Muslim inhabitants of North Africa and the European territories captured during the Islamic conquests of the Middle Ages – such as Spain, Sicily, and Malta. The Moors were not one ethnic group. They were Arabs, Berbers, Tuaregs, and other Muslim Africans. The word "Moor" comes from the Latin 'Maurus' = 'inhabitant of the Roman province of Mauretania' (portions of present-day Algeria, Morocco, and Spain).

"Moorish princes" – a 19th-century print

The fact that he was a *usurper* (an individual who seizes power by force), bothered Askia. He looked for a way to make his reign *legitimate* (in keeping with the law), and he found it. While on a Hajj journey, heading for Mecca, he stopped in Cairo to visit the *caliph* (ruler) of Egypt. Over there Askia announced that he officially resigned from being a king. That was it. He was no longer a king! He even put his crown in the hands of the caliph of Egypt, and let the caliph rule the Songhai Empire for... the whole three days of Askia's Egypt vacation! Three days later the caliph said he was done ruling the Songhai Empire and crowned Askia the Songhai king in a formal ceremony.

As Askia defeated and conquered his neighbors – the kingdom of Mossi, the kingdom of Mali, and many others, every time he gained territory, he married a woman from the ruling family of the conquered tribe. This helped to create alliances and make peace, but, as a result, most of Askia's kids were born to mothers whose countries had been destroyed and plundered by their dad. They grew up with mixed feelings about their father, and when Askia became old and blind – after 36 years on the throne – his kids couldn't wait to get rid of him.

"Timbuktu" – a 19th-century print

In 1528 his eldest son, Musa, overthrew Askia and seized power in the kingdom. Askia was locked in one of his palaces, but at least nobody bothered him there. Three years later, however, one of Askia's nephews killed Musa, seized the throne, and banished Askia to an island in the Niger River. From his exile, Askia watched in despair as his children tore the kingdom apart and killed one another, battling for the crown. But Askia was a fighter. Even in this hopeless situation he wasn't about to give up. A Mali legend says that when one of Askia's sons, Ismail, who was still loyal to him, visited him on the island, Askia put his hand on his son's arm and said: "Heavens! How can a powerful arm like this allow mosquitoes to eat me, and frogs to leap on me – abandoned here on the island?" With sadness, Ismail replied that he was powerless to help. Then Askia told him where to find a treasure of gold – enough to pay an army, and how to get in touch with men still loyal to Askia. With Ismail's help he overthrew his nephew and returned to his palace in the Songhai capital Gao. There, Askia gave his royal turban, his saber, and his throne to Ismail – in honor of his loyalty.

Askia was almost a hundred years old when he died in 1538. His tomb in Gao (present-day Mali) is a pyramid (56 feet / 17 meters high) made of dried mud and decorated with wooden spikes – the type of architecture typical in the Sahel of that era. It is still standing and is used as a mosque. All the materials for the tomb – the mud and the wood – had been brought by Askia from Mecca where he went on a Hajj pilgrimage.

Left: "A tribal chieftan from Gao" (1908-1912)
Below: Askia's tomb in Gao

King Afonso I

AFONSO I OF KONGO
1456 – 1542

Afonso I was the first king of Kongo to establish a close relationship with Portugal – a connection that lasted all the way to the 20th century. He was nicknamed "The Apostle of Kongo" for his role in introducing Christianity to his kingdom.

The West African Kingdom of Kongo was established in the 14th century. The *manikongo* (king) was elected by clans of the ruling families. He appointed officials who ruled the provinces of Kongo, collecting tribute from its many tribes in copper, iron, and slaves. **Cowrie shells** were used as *currency* (money).

In 1482, Portuguese explorer Diogo Cão, sailing down the coast of Africa in search of a passage to India, came to the mouth of the Congo River. He heard about the Kingdom of Kongo and traveled up the river to make contact with its king, Nzinga a Nkuwu, whose capital, Mbanza Kongo, was not far away. Cão sent presents to the king and on his way back captured a few Africans who he took with him to Portugal where they were trained to be interpreters. Eventually Portugal and Congo established diplomatic relations. King Nzinga a Nkuwu was baptized, took the name of the Portuguese king – João I – and invited Portuguese carpenters to build a church in his capital, Mbanza Kongo. The Portuguese helped the king defeat some enemy tribes, but once the Portuguese troops had loaded up their ships with enough slaves and ivory, they just left! And the Kongo kingdom went back to its traditional tribal religions and customs.

King João I

Cowrie shells

Cowrie are sea snails. The word 'cowrie' is of Indian origin, coming from the Hindi कौड़ी (kaudi). Italians called cowrie snails 'porcellana.' This is where our word 'porcelain' comes from. Both porcelain and cowrie shells are shiny and glass-like. The beauty of cowrie shells prompted many ancient peoples to use them as money – in India, Africa, Pacific islands, and other regions of the world. To buy ivory and slaves in West Africa, Europeans started importing billions of cowry shells from the coasts of the Indian Ocean. The shells cost very little in the Maldive Islands or Madagascar, but in West Africa they could buy a lot. Eventually, an over-supply of shells caused them to lose their value. In the Kingdom of Congo they also used the shells of the Olivella nana sea snail they called 'nzimbu.'

In 1509 King Nzinga died and his son Mvemba a Nzinga seized the throne after defeating one of his half-brothers who was opposed to the Portuguese influence and Christianity. Like his father, Mvemba a Nzinga adopted a Portuguese royal name – Afonso I. He claimed that during the battle with his brother and his supporters, he saw a vision of Saint James leading five "heavenly horsemen," as the cross of Constantine the Great appeared in the sky. Even though enemies outnumbered Afonso's troops, they fled the battlefield, and Afonso's half-brother was killed. In honor of this miracle, the Portuguese king granted Afonso a royal coat of arms depicting Constantine's cross and the arms of the five "heavenly knights."

Saint James and Constantine the Great

Saint James was one of the Twelve Apostles of Jesus. His name also appears in English translations of the Bible as Jacob. James and his brother John were nicknamed "Sons of Thunder" for their uncompromising fighting spirit. In Medieval Spain and Portugal St.James was viewed as the **patron saint** (spiritual protector/leader) of the **Reconquista** – the military campaign of the Spanish Christian kingdoms to liberate the Iberian Peninsula from the Moors – North African Muslim warlords. The place name 'Santiago' and the personal name 'Diego' came from the Latin 'Sancti Iacobi' ('of Saint Jacob / James').

Constantine the Great was the first Roman Emperor (AD 306 - 337) to convert to Christianity. Once, on a march toward a battlefield, Constantine had a vision. He saw a cross of light in the sky above the sun, and the words in Latin, 'In Hoc Signo Vinces' ('With this sign you shall win'). Soon, when facing his enemies in battle, Constantine put the **Christogram**, an early Christian symbol, on his banners and on his soldiers' shields. The Christogram is the Greek letters Chi (kai) and Rho (ro) – XP – the first two letters of the word 'Christ' in Greek – ΧΡΙΣΤΟΣ (Hristos).

Portuguese fort St. Anthony on the 'Gold Coast' of Africa, 1515 (Ghana)

Europeans join in the Africa slave trade

By the mid-13th century, Portugal expelled the North African Muslim invaders from its territory and was free to use its resources for exploration and trade. The Portuguese monarchs were especially interested in the gold of Africa. That gold could finance their expeditions to India. In the 15th century Prince Henry the Navigator set a goal of undermining the **trans-Saharan** (across the Sahara desert) gold trade of the Muslims by sending ships down the coast of Africa to buy gold directly from the Africans. Over a few decades the Portuguese established trading posts on the **Gold Coast** (present-day Ghana) where the gold was brought for sale from deep inland. But there was a problem: How to pay for the gold?

The Gold Coast is located in the rainforest belt of Africa. In the equatorial heat European cloth wasn't in demand. Horses, so highly prized in the Sahel and in the savanna regions, were of little value in this heavily-forested region, plus they were killed by trypanosomiasis (sleeping sickness) – the disease carried by the **tsetse fly** common in tropical Africa. Native warriors were interested in buying firearms, but their sale to Africans was at that point prohibited by the Pope. However, native West African societies used slave labor and purchased slaves. So the Portuguese started buying slaves on markets along what became known as the **Slave Coast** (Equatorial Africa) and exchanging them for gold in Ghana. By the end of the 15th century the Portuguese brought half a ton of gold a year from Africa for sale in Europe – all paid for by the sale of African slaves to other Africans. It was only much later, in the mid-16th century, when the Portuguese started purchasing slaves for their plantations in Brazil.

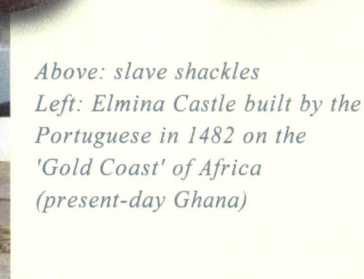

Above: slave shackles
Left: Elmina Castle built by the Portuguese in 1482 on the 'Gold Coast' of Africa (present-day Ghana)

King Afonso signed an agreement with the Portuguese granting the Kingdom of Kongo independence as long as it supplied slaves to Portuguese traders. Slavery was common in Kongo, like everywhere in Africa, but buying and selling slaves was not. Most slaves were prisoners of war. In 1526 Portuguese slave traders were caught purchasing Africans who were not prisoners of war, but Kongo farmers. To make sure this would never happen again, Afonso created a special branch of his government to oversee the slave trade. A few times he tried to ban the slave trade altogether, allowing only one Portuguese ship per year to enter the Kongo – carrying supplies for churches. But the Portuguese said NO to that. They also demanded that all European priests and monks working in Kongo be paid for with... slaves! Churches needed Portuguese goods such as candles, decor, and clothing, but the 'nzimbu' shells and cowry shells – the Kongo currency – were only good to buy local African goods and food. So slaves were used as money.

King Afonso established the first school system in Kongo. Portuguese monks trained local tribesmen as teachers, and these teachers were sent all around the kingdom to organize schools for boys and girls where they studied reading and writing in Latin and Portuguese, and the basics of Christianity. Some of these schools attracted as many as 1000 students! Afonso also sent his son and dozens of the kids of tribal chiefs to study in Portugal and at *the Vatican*. They were trained as interpreters, priests, and royal ambassadors. The Kingdom of Kongo paid for their education with slaves.

The Vatican

Vatican City is the headquarters of the Roman Catholic Church and home to the Pope. It is currently a city-state located in the middle of Rome, Italy.

Right: "Don Miguel de Castro, Emissary (a diplomat) of Congo," 1643; Below: African traders selling ivory to the Europeans (19th-century photo)

Most of what we know about the life of King Afonso comes from the many letters he wrote to Portuguese kings and officials in the Vatican. For example, in his letter to the King of Portugal, Manuel I (October 5, 1514), King Afonso described his struggle against traditional tribal beliefs – mainly cults of the spirits of ancestors, or elders. Their *idols* – statues of ancestors – were worshiped in 'sacred forests.' The king wanted to destroy them, but was afraid his subjects would rebel. He asked Fernao de Melo, the Portuguese governor of São Tomé (a Portuguese colony on an island in the Gulf of Guinea), to send him some ships "with bombards and blunderbusses" (cannons and shotguns). To pay for the weapons, Afonso sent to the governor "one thousand five hundred copper shackles and one hundred and fifty slaves."

But King Afonso did not get what he paid for. He bitterly complained to Manuel I about the corrupt Portuguese officials in Africa:
"Most high and mighty Prince and Lord, we, Dom Afonso, by the grace of God, King of Kongo, commend ourselves to your Royal Highness as to a king and lord who we dearly love... Greed took hold of Fernao de Melo. He sent us a ship carrying no merchandise, except for a bed cover, a carpet, a curtain fringe and a glass carafe... Fernao de Melo said that he did not have bombards and blunderbusses, but that, if we were to send him more merchandise, he would purchase them... So we sent him eight hundred shackles and fifty slaves for him and his wife, fifty shackles for his son, thirty for the captain and twenty for the clerk.... We waited in vain for a year... And then we began to burn all the idols ourselves..."

The Portuguese used the West Coast of Africa as a place where they deported convicted criminals. Many of them ended up working as sailors, soldiers, captains, and traders, bringing the ruthless habits of the criminal world into the dealings between the Portuguese and the Africans. Here is a typical story of theft and disrespect, again described by King Afonso in another letter to Manuel I: "We sent our cousin, our brother, and our nephews with a letter for Your Highness. We sent to you seven hundred shackles, many slaves, parrots, other animals as well as several civets [cat-like mammals]... When Estevao da Rocha [Portuguese ship captain] saw all of the merchandise on the ship, he took the letter we had written to Your Highness and threw it in the mud. He also broke the arm of our nephew who refused to leave the ship, threw all of our relatives overboard, and fled with all the gifts we intended to send to Your Highness."

Practically every instance of interaction between the Africans and the Portuguese ended in a disaster. King Afonso requested the Portuguese to bring **masons** (stone workers), carpenters, and clothes makers to Kongo. The workers arrived, but their attitude wasn't better than that of the Portuguese officials and captains. "We asked the masons to build us a stone house in which we could live with the Queen," wrote King Afonso. "They built its foundations for over a year. They went there each day to lay just a stone or two and then returned to their homes, but this did not prevent them from coming to me asking for money... They wanted servants, so we gave them money to buy slaves, but soon they told us that the slaves had fled. They also came to tell us that they had no wine. They worked on this house for five years and they could not complete it... We gave fifty skins to a shoemaker who had come here, so that he would **tan** them [**tanning** = processing animal skins to make leather] and make us some shoes, twenty of goat, twenty of sheep, and twenty others from animals native to the country. He didn't know how to tan the skins and didn't want to work. In addition he wasted everything we had given him and made only five pairs of shoes. The tile maker never wanted to make either tiles or bricks. Each day, we gave him money and sent him to work, but he never went. These artisans taught their professions to none of our servants. On the contrary, if these servants went to watch them work in order to learn, they were beaten so many times that they fled and no longer wished to return."

Slaves remained the main export of the Kingdom of Kongo until the mid-19th century when Portugal banned the slave trade. European traders in Kongo switched from slaves to buying wax, ivory, peanuts, and – as the car industry emerged – rubber for car tires. In 1884 at the Conference of Berlin, European colonial powers divided between themselves most of Central Africa. Portugal claimed the Kingdom of Kongo, and in 1914, after it rebelled against colonization, the Portuguese abolished the Kongo monarchy and replaced it with direct colonial rule from Lisbon.

Manuel III, the last King of Kongo

Tango and Zombie

These two words come from African Bantu languages that were spoken in the Kingdom of Kongo and Angola. "Zombie" comes from the word zumbi/djumbi - "ghost" and was brought by African slaves to Haiti where it came to mean 'corpse that came alive.' 'Tango' comes from the root 'tamgu' = to dance. It was brought by African slaves to South America where, originally, it was the name of an African dance performed to a drumbeat.

Queen Nzinga
1583 – 1663

Queen Nzinga Mbande ruled the kingdoms of Ndongo and Matamba on the Kwanza river in present-day Angola. There are contradictory views on Queen Nzinga's role in the history of her people. Some historians portray her as an anti-colonial resistance hero who defended her people against the Portuguese slave traders. Others accuse her of helping the Europeans develop and grow the slave trade in Angola. Slavery existed in Angola. Prisoners or war were routinely enslaved and occasionally sold from tribe to tribe. But European and Arab slave traders took this a step further. They encouraged native African chiefs to raid their neighbors specifically for the purpose of capturing slaves. They did it through buying unlimited numbers of slaves, paying for them with European and Silk Road goods highly prized in Africa.

Nzinga was a leader of rare courage, and she was a brilliant negotiator. But it is unlikely that she became a ruler thanks to these skills, or even thanks to her royal origin. Her father was the ***ngola*** (king) of the Mbundu, the people of the Ndongo region, and he treated her as an equal to his sons. She was trained in axe combat and other warrior skills, and was allowed to be present at war councils. Her dad let Portuguese Catholic missionaries teach Nzinga the Portuguese language. She learned to read and write. The laws of the Mbundu specifically prohibited women from taking royal titles, and that was the main reason Nzinga was allowed so close to the throne. She wasn't a threat to her brothers. Following the custom of the Mbundu royals, Nzinga wasn't married, but she had a boyfriend, her favorite slave, and they had a son.

In 1575, 8 years before Nzinga was born, the Portuguese founded the colony of Luanda right next to the Ndongo lands, and started buying slaves. Plantations and mines in the vast Portuguese colony of Brazil needed workers. Dozens of thousands of Africans were shipped there every year.

Queen Nzinga Statue in Luanda, Angola

The Portuguese didn't tolerate any pushback from the native tribes, and at any opportunity burned their villages, captured tribespeople for sale in South America, and built forts deeper and deeper into the tribal lands. So the Kingdom of Ndongo was shrinking, losing to both the Portuguese and to their rival, the Kingdom of Kongo, to the North. The Portuguese also paid the Imbangala, bands of warriors who migrated toward the coast from Central Africa, to plunder the Mbundu tribes and supply prisoners to the slave market in Luanda. The Imbangala practiced cannibalism. The Mbundu were terrified of them and resented that Ndongo kings were not able to protect them from this new threat. Some tribes stopped paying tribute to the royal family and sided with the Portuguese.

In 1617, when Nzinga was 35, her dad died, and her half-brother Mbandi became ngola, the king of the Mbundu. Ndongo society was *matrilineal*. People belonged to the clan of their mother, not their father. So while the ngola, or king, represented his own clan, his kids belonged to the clans of their mothers. And when the king died, all those clans had a claim to the throne! As a result, the Ndongo monarchy was *elective* rather than a *hereditary* – the king didn't inherit the throne, but was elected by the ruling families. However, because royal power constantly passed from clan to clan, the king could never fully rely on any of the Ndongo clans. To keep their own relatives away from the throne, Mbundu kings surrounded themselves with talented men from defeated tribes – often prisoners of war – appointing them military commanders and court officials. Europeans referred to these foreigners as 'slaves.' Nzinga's mom was from one of these 'slave' families. While Nzinga and Mbandi had the same father, they belonged to different clans – those of their mothers, and, by the Mbundu laws they weren't even considered relatives.

As Mbandi became king, he made his goal to strengthen the crumbling royal power by killing any of his relatives whose families were potential rivals for the Ndongo crown. He started by murdering his oldest half-brother and his whole family, and ended by killing Nzinga's son, even though the kid's dad was a slave with no claim to the throne. In grief and shock, Nzinga escaped to the nearby Kingdom of Matamba. Yet only 5 years later, in 1622, according to the Portuguese, Nzinga came to Luanda to negotiate with the Portuguese governor as an ambassador representing her brother Mbandi... How did that happen?

Killing his rivals helped Mbandi to claim a few years on the throne, but barely. He had hardly any leadership abilities and was a talentless military commander. Even though he attracted the Imbangala on his side, he was losing badly to the Portuguese.

It's possible that Mbandi asked Nzinga, who spoke fluent Portuguese, to help him negotiate with the colonists, but many historians believe that, while in exile, Nzinga managed to build an alliance of families who opposed Mbandi. Well, one way or another, these families overthrew Mbandi either before or after Nzinga's trip to Luanda in 1622.

Nzinga immediately became a celebrity among the Portuguese. Unlike other African royalty who wore European clothes when meeting with the colonial authorities, Nzinga came to Luanda dressed in the style of her native tribe, her outfit decorated with feathers and jewels. Governor João Correia de Sousa received her in a room with only one chair which he took. He offered Nzinga to sit on a carpet spread on the floor, but Nzinga knew that this put her in a subordinate position, so she ordered one of her female slaves to go down on her hands and knees, and sat on the slave's back. By the end of the meeting, Nzinga rose to leave, but the slave remained on the floor. Noticing the curious looks of the Portuguese, Nzinga informed Governor de Sousa that the slave girl was a gift for him because Ndongo royalty "never sit on the same chair twice!"

Portuguese engraving: Queen Nzinga

An even greater surprise was the agreement Nzinga negotiated with Governor de Sousa. First she stated that the Kingdom of Ndongo was far from being defeated by the Portuguese, and threatened to continue war unless the Portuguese remove their forts from the Ndongo lands. Then she declared that her people would no longer pay tribute to Portugal and demanded the Portuguese cease slave raids in Ndongo. Hearing that, de Sousa was likely about to fall out of his chair in shock. But Nzinga knew that what she requested wasn't free. What did she offer in return? The Kingdom of Ndongo would fight the enemy tribes and supply prisoners of war as slaves to Luanda – in any numbers – as long as the Portuguese pay for them with European weapons. The Kingdom of Ndongo would no longer protect slaves who escaped from the Portuguese – all captured runaways would be returned to Luanda. Portuguese slave traders would be welcome in Ndongo as long as they were not enslaving the native Mbundu.

Catholic missionaries would be welcome anywhere on the lands controlled by Ndongo. Finally, as a gesture of good will, Nzinga offered to convert to Catholicism. The agreement was finalized, and Nzinga was baptized in Luanda, adopting a Christian name, 'Anna,' and the Luanda Governor's last name – 'de Sousa.' Her godparents were the governor and his wife.

From Luanda, Nzinga returned to the Kingdom of Ndongo. Two years later her brother Mbandi died under mysterious circumstances, and Nzinga proclaimed herself the Queen of Ndongo. But Mbandi's family was still a threat: Mbandi had a 7-year-old son, and one of the most ferocious Imbangala warlords, Kaza, trained him in martial arts and was sworn to protect him. While Nzinga was trying to figure out how to get rid of Mbandi's son, a new threat arose. Governor de Sousa left Africa, and the new Portuguese governor broke the agreement with Nzinga. He refused to remove Portuguese forts from the Ndongo lands, and, thinking that a woman wouldn't last long on the Ndongo throne, he started supporting Hari a Kiluanje, a Mbundu chief who came from one of the ruling families. Nzinga sent troops to capture and kill Hari a Kiluanje, but they were defeated, and many among Nzinga's warriors and chiefs defected to Hari a Kiluanje. To replace them with loyal supporters, Nzinga started offering asylum to slaves escaping from the Portuguese plantations. In response, in 1626 the Portuguese declared war on the Kingdom of Ndongo.

Nzinga's army fought from its base, located on islands in the Kwanza River, but suffered a defeat. Nzinga escaped captivity only because the Portuguese were more interested in capturing as many of her warriors as they could (for sale into slavery) than in taking their queen prisoner.

Portuguese Fort of Massangano, Angola, built in 1583

Nzinga tried to negotiate with the Portuguese again. She agreed to pay tribute and even sent them a 'gift' of 400 slaves, but the Portuguese beheaded her messenger and told her to surrender. Nzinga continued suffering defeats and was eventually chased out of her kingdom with only 200 loyal warriors. When it looked like everything was lost, suddenly, Nzinga received a word from the Imbangala. Kaza, the guardian of Mbandi's son, was interested in an alliance and offered her a position as a female Imbangala chieftain called a 'tembanza.' Portuguese sources described this alliance as a 'marriage,' but actually it was just a way of creating alliances by bringing female leaders into Imbangala military camps. The ritual of becoming the tembanza involved the cannibalistic 'blood oath' (drinking human blood)! In addition, Nzinga agreed to abandon her Mbundu customs and beliefs, and in return had her warriors trained in the Imbangala war arts. But the friendship between Kaza and Nzinga didn't last. While living in Kaza's camp, Nzinga had Mbandi's son killed. Kaza held it against her, and soon the Imbangala took the side of the Portuguese.

By 1631 Nzinga's army had grown and her forces started attacking the Portuguese again. Also, she hired some of Kaza's Imbangala warriors to help her invade and conquer the Kingdom of Matamba where Nzinga had once lived in exile. Unlike Ndongo, Matamba welcomed female rulers, so Nzinga proclaimed herself the queen of Matamba. But the Imbangala were *mercenaries* – soldiers-for-hire – and they wouldn't help Nzinga for free. To pay them, Nzinga began selling Matambans to the Dutch slave traders who operated on the territory of Kongo. Soon the Dutch were buying about 13 thousand slaves from Nzinga every year. To replace the Matambans sold to the Dutch, Nzinga resettled tribespeople from Ndongo to Matamba.

In 1641 the Dutch West India Company drove the Portuguese out of Luanda and made an alliance with Nzinga. By 1648 Nzinga had succeeded in returning most of Ndongo lands to her control. But there were losses as well. The Imbangala captured some portions of the Kingdom of Matamba. Also, the Portuguese captured Nzinga's sister Kambu who carried an archive of letters written by Nzinga and her family. From these letters they learned that Nzinga's other sister, Funji, who was in Portuguese captivity, had been spying on the Portuguese and sending Nzinga tips about their plans and troops movement. Enraged, the Portuguese governor executed Funji by drowning her in the Kwanza River. In revenge Nzinga laid siege to the Portuguese fort of Massangano cutting off the Portuguese from their slave trade routes and plantations. But the tide was about to turn again.

In 1648 Portuguese reinforcements arrived in Massangano. The fort was still under siege – by the Dutch, since Nzinga's troops were away defending Matamba. The Portuguese bombarded the Dutch troops from the sea. Unwilling to sacrifice his men for just another slave-trading outpost, the Dutch commander asked for peace and agreed to leave Angola immediately – without even sending a word to Nzinga! So when Nzinga's forces came to help the Dutch at Massangano, they saw the Dutch fleet on the horizon sailing for Europe, and faced the Portuguese ready for battle. So the war continued... and Nzinga won. Her troops held the Portuguese, pinning them down in the coastal region.

In 1644 Nzinga's warriors captured a Portuguese Catholic priest. Conversations with him made Nzinga rethink her dismissive attitude to Christianity. She became curious about the unifying power of Christian faith – especially when adopted as a state religion. In 1648 two

Queen Nzinga and captured missionaries;
Below: Tribal masks (Angola) used in native religious rituals

Spanish monks, Catholic missionaries, were captured. One of them became Nzinga's personal friend and secretary, and helped her establish a correspondence with Pope Alexander VII. Suddenly Nzinga realized that Christians could be her new loyal supporters, and started relying more and more on Africans who converted to Christianity. She placed crosses on the sites considered holy in Ndongo, built churches, and hired Christian Africans as her advisors. She banned the practice of having *concubines* (slave-wives) and married her own favorite slave boyfriend in a Christian ceremony. When the Mbundu protested this change, Nzinga encouraged Europeans at her court to burn down temples dedicated to the native religions, and sold protesters into slavery.

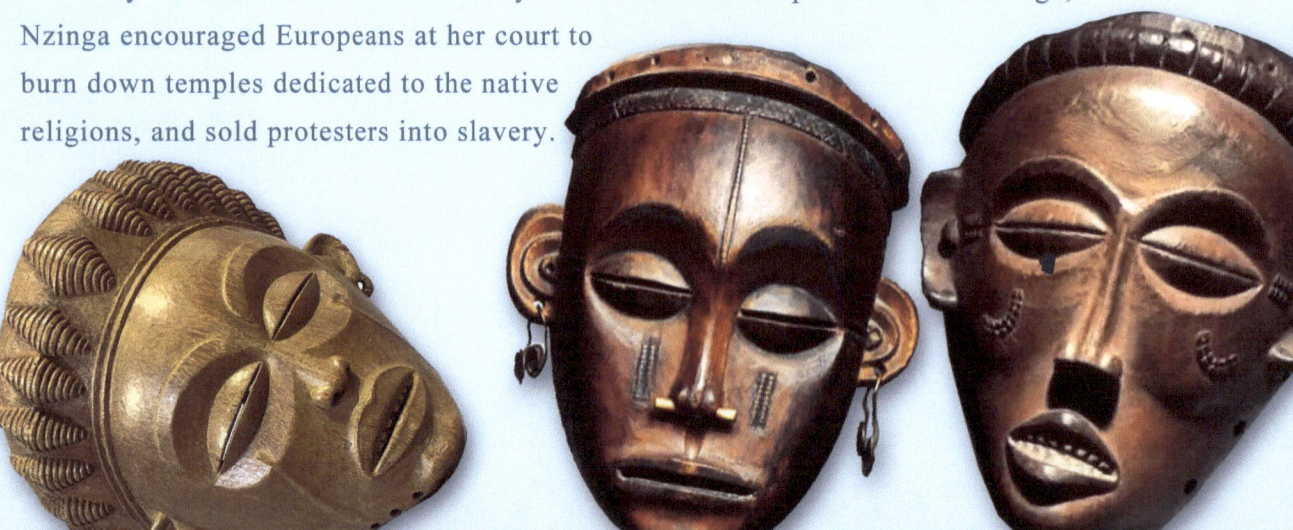

The tragic side of Nzinga's rule was her dependence on the support of outsiders. Neither her military successes, not the wealth Nzinga obtained from the slave trade, gave her an authority that was fully accepted in either of her two kingdoms. In Ndongo she was viewed as a usurper with no rightful claim to the throne, and in Matamba she was a foreigner and a conqueror. When the Dutch were gone, Nzinga realized that the Portuguese were a lesser threat than her own subjects that didn't recognize her claim to the throne. So, in the 1650s, she reached out to the Portuguese for peace. She was already in her 70s, and her war against Portugal had been going on for 25 years. Another reason she wanted peace was the fact that her sister Kambu was still a prisoner of the Portuguese. She had lived in captivity for 30 years. Meanwhile, she was the only person to whom Nzinga wanted to leave the throne. The Portuguese understood this and demanded a giant ransom for Kambu. Eventually she was released and negotiations began. The peace treaty specified new borders, and placed the main Portuguese slave market in Nzinga's capital, making her the main supplier of slaves for the Portuguese. Nzinga died in her 80s. After her death Kambu became queen of Ndongo and Matamba.

Vintage prints, 18-19th century: View of Luanda; native African slave traders; Portuguese "feitoria" (slave trading post); a 20 kwanzas coin (Angola, 2014) featuring Nzinga

SHAKA ZULU

1787 – 1828

Shaka Zulu was an African conqueror-king whose conquests reshaped the tribal map of southeastern Africa. During the 12 years of his rule, Shaka created a powerful Zulu nation out of many scattered tribes. But the cost of his nation-building was a tragedy – over a million Africans perished as a result of Shaka's wars, and the mass migration of tribes escaping the Zulu invasion.

Zulus belong to the tribes of Central Africa who speak *Bantu* languages. The Bantu tribes knew how to smelt iron – their spears had iron tips. They cultivated cattle and crops such as grain, squash, and sweet potatoes. But the Bantu didn't know how to rotate crops to keep the land fertile. It was quickly exhausted, crops became smaller and the Bantu tribes had to move to a new area. This made them a *semi-nomadic* people – settled for some years, then migrating to a new place.

By the 18th century the Zulus were just a small clan of a large Bantu tribe – no more than 1500 people. In the Zulu language the word "Zulu" meant 'the Heavens,' or 'weather.'

An assegai (a Zulu spear) and a Zulu neckace

Crop Rotation

When they grow the same crop year after year, for example, wheat, the soil where it grows becomes poor in the nutrients that nourish wheat, such as nitrogen. So the amount of grain reaped becomes smaller and smaller with every harvest. But if, on the same field, they sow wheat one year, and beans the next year, the level of the nitrogen in the soil stays the same, because the roots of the beans are home to bacteria that produce nitrogen compounds. Alternating crops in this way is called 'crop rotation.'

Wealthy Bantu tribesmen had a few wives, and tribal chiefs, a few dozen wives. Among the wives of a Bantu chief there was always the 'great wife' – a daughter of another chief, whose eldest son would inherit the wealth and the power of his dad. However, to marry a daughter of another tribal chief, it was necessary to give the bride's family a huge number of cattle – as a payment for the bride. So by the time a Bantu tribal chief had enough cattle to pay for a 'great wife,' he already had a few 'regular' wives and lots of kids. And by the time he died, the 'great wife''s son was likely still a kid, while his older half-brothers were adults with influence and warrior skills. This regularly caused clashes and wars over tribal leadership and inheritance.

Shaka was a son of the Zulu clan leader – the king – but his mom, Nandi, was not the king's 'great wife,' so Shaka had no claim to the throne. The meaning of his name, 'Shaka,' was a 'parasite beetle'. At the age of 6, like all Bantu boys, Shaka was sent to the fields to herd his father's cattle. He worked from sunrise to sunset, but one day he got distracted, and at that moment his dog killed a lamb in his herd. Shaka's dad was furious and kicked Shaka and his mom out of the royal camp. Nandi found shelter with her native Langeni tribe where Shaka was bullied and grew up lonely and bitter. As a teenager, however, Shaka turned out to be 6'2 tall (1m 87cm) – much taller than most Bantu men – and showed remarkable strength. Suddenly his dad's tribe was interested in him as a warrior, and so, around 1802, Shaka was sent to learn military skills with the Mtetwa clan, famous for training great fighters.

*A Zulu **kraal** (a village, a compound) by George French Angas, 1849*
a Zulu knobkerrie (a club, weapon)

The chief of the Mtetwa, Dingiswayo, carried a gun and rode a horse. Neither guns, nor horses were known to the Zulu and the Mtetwa. Tribespeople feared and nearly worshiped Dingiswayo. The gun and the horse had once belonged to Dr. Andrew Cowan, a British army doctor and explorer of southern Africa who had been killed by one of the Bantu tribes. The Bantu believed that the white colonists were sea monsters living in giant shells (their ships!) and feeding on elephant tusks (the ivory Europeans purchased for export to Europe). Around that time Dingiswayo's father died. Dingiswayo purchased Dr. Cowan's gun and his horse, and returned to his homeland to claim the throne.

A Zulu warrior, by George French Angas, 1849

There was something else interesting about Dingiswayo. The meaning of his name is "the wanderer." As a young man he conspired with his brother to kill their dad – an old tribal chief who was just too slow to die! Their dad discovered the plot. One of the brothers was killed, the other escaped and lived in exile, where he adopted the name "Dingiswayo" – "the wanderer." During his exile he came in contact with Portuguese colonists and had the opportunity to observe their military training. He noticed that in combat European soldiers moved in *formations*, and that their troops had tactics and a *chain of command* – soldiers followed the orders of their unit commanders, and the unit commanders followed the orders of senior commanders. This was very different from Bantu warriors who typically attacked in a disorganized crowd, each man fighting without coordination within the group. Dingiswayo used these observations to improve the military training and the warfare tactics of his tribe. And that's where Shaka Zulu's spectacular military success began.

Dingiswayo was a talented leader. He decided to stop the constant fighting between tribes by conquering as many of them as he could and forcing them to live in peace with one another. He followed through with this idea and conquered 30 tribes. The defeated clans were allowed to keep their land, but had to send a certain number of young warriors to Dingiswayo's army.

Military formation

*A military formation is a group of soldiers who coordinate their actions with one another and move together in an organized way that was designed and rehearsed in advance. For example, the most famous military formation in Ancient Rome was the **testudo** ('tortoise' in Latin). The formation was made of 27 soldiers who held their shields over their heads and out to the sides – like a tortoise shell – to protect themselves from the enemy arrows. The Roman attack formation was the **wedge** (Latin: 'cuneus,' also known as 'caput porcinum' – the 'pig's head'). Soldiers advanced in a group shaped as a triangle. The goal of the 'wedge' was to force apart the enemy lines.*

This was another idea that Shaka Zulu learned from his teacher – organizing society around the army. Mtetwa warriors were divided into units by age, and those who displayed courage and military talent were promoted to leadership even if their family was poor and of low status in the tribe. Bantu warriors were armed with light steel-tipped spears – *assegais*, and carried large shields made from cowhide. The Bantu were familiar with the bow and arrow, but none of the wood available in their region was strong and flexible enough for a bow. The battles usually started with throwing assegai and ended in hand-to-hand combat. Occasionally battles were replaced with a one-on-one fight between the 2 strongest warriors. Women and kids often gathered to observe battles, and, even when their side lost, their life was not in danger – they were allowed to run away.

Shaka Zulu spent 6 years in Dingiswayo's army. For courage and tactical skill he was made a commander of his Mtetwa "regiment." From his first days in the army Shaka wanted to make warfare more destructive, more deadly.

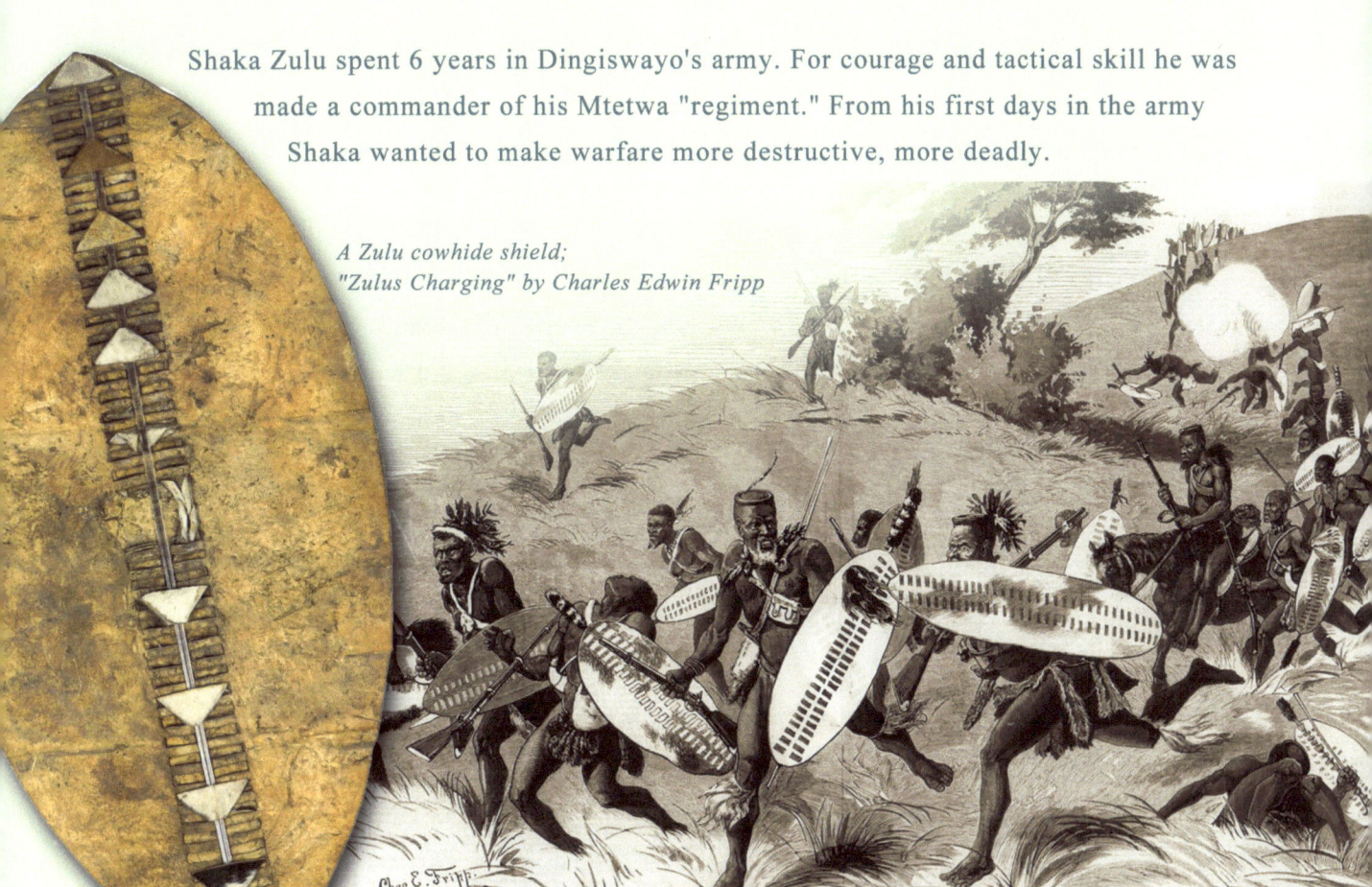

A Zulu cowhide shield;
"Zulus Charging" by Charles Edwin Fripp

Throwing spears rarely killed anyone. So Shaka invented a short stabbing spear with a broad blade – for close combat. It was similar to a sword. He also preferred to fight barefoot. He felt the cowhide sandals of Bantu warriors slowed him down. The first time Shaka tested his new fighting technique was in a battle against the Buthelezi tribe. The Buthelezi chief challenged the strongest man from Dingiswayo's troops to a one-on-one fight, and, when Shaka stepped forward, everyone expected them to exchange throwing spears. But Shaka rushed at the Buthelezi chief, forced his shield to the side and killed him with his new stabbing spear. The Buthelezi warriors signaled surrender by dropping their shields and running away. Normally that would have been the end of the battle, but Shaka ordered his men to chase and slaughter the Buthelezi. It was the first instance of what would become Shaka-style warfare – ruthless, destroying the enemy to the last man.

Shaka organized his troops in a formation known as 'head, horns, and chest.' The 'head' was the assault unit of the strongest warriors. The 'horns' were groups of warriors advancing in a semicircle – trying to encircle the enemy. The 'chest' was the main body of the army. Shaka also mobilized teenagers, 15-16 year old boys, to carry weapons and water for his warriors. He demanded what he called a 'red attack' – the 'total war' that would destroy not just the enemy troops, but also their civilian population – women, kids, and the old. This was one point where Shaka and Dingiswayo disagreed. Dingiswayo defended the humane attitude to civilians, and often 'forgave' enemy chiefs if they pledged loyalty to him.

Meanwhile, there was an unexpected outcome of the war with the Buthelezi. The Zulu clan of Shaka's father was an ally of the defeated Buthelezi. So now the Zulus were ruled by Dingiswayo, and everyone knew that it was only a matter of time before Shaka, the Zulu king's son, would assume the leadership of the Zulus. Indeed, that is exactly what happened. Dingiswayo told the Zulu king to make Shaka his heir. Shaka's dad pretended to agree, but a few days later he declared Shaka's younger half-brother Sigujana the future king. In 1816 the old king died and Sigujana claimed the throne, but was soon killed by another half-brother loyal to Shaka, and Shaka became the king of the Zulus. Right away Shaka started organizing the Zulu clan into a war machine, assembling men into regiments and training them. He also built himself a ***kraal*** – a compound of royal houses for his wives and kids. Bizarrely, he called it Bulawayo – "The Place of Killing."

Shaka's troops were enthusiastic about the new stabbing spears, but when it came to fighting barefoot they rebelled, because the Zulu lands were notorious for thorny plants called the 'devil thorn.' To crush his men's resistance, Shaka covered the town square with the 'devil thorn' plants and ordered his warriors to stamp those thorns into the dirt with their bare feet. Anyone who resisted would be killed on the spot, he said. "My slayers are at hand." A squad of professional executioners with clubs stood at the edge of the square. Some Zulus protested and were immediately clubbed to death. Once all the thorns were beaten into the ground, Shaka ordered an unlimited amount of beer and beef to be served to his terrified troops.

"Zulu Warriors" by Richard Caton Woodville, 1892

The first target of Shaka's war machine was his mom's tribe, the Langenis – those kids who bullied him when he and his mom Nandi lived in exile. The Zulu army surrounded the Langeni camp. All Langenis were dragged out of their huts onto the town square. There, Shaka sorted them into 2 groups – those whose insults and unkind attitude to his mother he couldn't forgive, and those who could be forgiven. From the second group only one man ended up forgiven. He had given Shaka's mom a grinding stone to make flour. He was let go. Everyone else was clubbed to death.

A Zulu attack (19th-century print)

The next target was the Buthelezi tribe ("forgiven" by Dingiswayo). Their army was surrounded on the battlefield and ruthlessly slaughtered. Then the Zulus rushed to the Buthelezi kraal – their tribal village – killed all the elderly, captured all the women and kids and burned the Buthelezi huts to the ground. Out of the 100 women the Zulus captured, the most beautiful ones were to become Shaka's wives, and the rest were trained to be soldiers. However, when it came to marriage, Shaka was suddenly filled with fear. What if his kids try to kill him like Dingiswayo and many other tribal princes attempted to do, to get rid of their elderly dads? So Shaka decided to never marry and never have children. His Buthelezi "brides" were to be called his "sisters". They lived with his mom and were treated as house servants. Shaka also prohibited his soldiers from getting married and having kids. Anyone who disobeyed was executed. Eventually he allowed some of them to start families, but only if they displayed bravery in battle and were particularly trusted by Shaka.

A year after Shaka became the king of the Zulus, his army grew from 400 to 2000 warriors and the Zulu-controlled territory quadrupled. Shaka and his army fought against Dingiswayo's enemies, but Shaka was angry at Dingiswayo who always 'forgave' the defeated tribes instead of destroying them. Once Dingiswayo invited Shaka on a joint military campaign against the Ndwandwe tribe and its chief Zwide. The two armies were supposed to surround the Ndwandwa, but for some reason Shaka and his troops were late arriving to the battlefield. As a result Zwide captured and executed Dingiswayo. Shaka's enemies were convinced he betrayed Dingiswayo to get rid of him. Even though the Ndwandwe warriors were highly-skilled, they were no match for Shaka's army. They were defeated and Zwide perished.

Unlike his teacher Dingiswayo, Shaka didn't 'forgive' the conquered tribes. He killed their rulers, broke them into separate clans, moved them away from their land, and made them accept the Zulu identity. They were forced to become members of the Zulu nation and its soldiers. By the 1820s Shaka's army was gigantic. All his soldiers did was train and fight. There were not enough men left in Zululand to plant crops or raise cattle, so the army had to feed themselves by plundering conquered tribes. This fueled endless wars and caused a chain of migrations. Thousands of people escaped the Zulus, pushing other tribes from their lands. In Bantu this series of events is called the Mfecane – "the Crushing."

A vintage photo of a Zulu warrior

Breaking with Zulu tradition, Shaka refused to share power with the Zulu religious leaders – 'magicians' and 'witch hunters.' Like all Zulus, Shaka believed in witchcraft and followed dozens of rules that were supposed to protect him against evil spirits and witches. The problem was, the 'witch hunters' could declare anyone a 'witch' and get them killed, so they had a lot of power over tribespeople. The 'witch hunters' – mostly women – were called *isangomas*. When the tribe suffered from a drought or a disease, isangomas held a witch-hunting ceremony called the 'sniffing out.' They walked through a crowd of the Zulus with whips made from the tails of gnu antilopes. They were followed by the 'slayers,' professional executioners. Whoever was hit by a whip of an isangoma was declared a 'witch' and instantly dragged away by the 'slayers' to be executed. Shaka came up with a plan to trick

A photo of a Zulu chief, 1902

isangomas and destroy them. One night, with the help of a trusted servant, Shaka splashed cow blood on the wall of his hut. In the morning the presence of the blood was proclaimed to be a result of evil witchcraft, and isangomas were called to "sniff out" the evildoers. Predictably, isangomas accused many of Shaka's close advisors and commanders – who didn't respect witch hunters. Only one witch hunter suspected the trap and didn't accuse anyone. When Shaka asked that witch hunter who had splashed blood on the royal hut, the isangoma said, "Heavens" – using the word that was one of the titles of the Zulu king. Shaka let that isangoma go, and executed all the rest.

Another group with which Bantu chiefs traditionally shared power were the ***elders*** – older men from influential families. To destroy their authority Shaka ordered them to wear women's skirts made of monkey skins. The elders were ridiculed wherever they went, and once the Zulus lost any respect for them, Shaka had most of them executed.

In 1823 Henry Fynn, a 30-year-old English trader, sailed with a couple companions to Natal in southeastern Africa, in search of a place to start a British settlement. There he ran into the Zulu troops coming home from a military campaign. Fynn could speak some Bantu, and the Zulus invited him to go with them and meet Shaka.

In his diary Fynn reported his conversations with Shaka and described the Zulu customs he saw. When he told Shaka about King George of England, and mentioned that the king was married, but had only one wife, Shaka said marrying even one wife was a huge blunder showing that the English king lacked wisdom. Henry Fynn gave Shaka a magnifying glass as a gift and taught him to make fire by focusing sunlight on one spot. Shaka immediately tested it by burning a hole in the hand of one of his servants. Fynn wrote that the servant "writhed in pain, but didn't make a sound."

In public Shaka always appeared with 'praise singers' who loudly proclaimed his greatness, calling him "Sitting Thunder," "He Who Is Equal to A Thousand Men," or "The Great Elephant." When Shaka spoke, people around him exclaimed "Yebo, Baba!" ('Yes, Father!'). Every morning crowds of Zulus gathered to see Shaka's bath. While servants washed Shaka in the river, Shaka talked to his military commanders and guests, decided court cases and always ordered a few executions to keep his subjects filled with terror. Shaka's biographer, E.A. Ritter quotes the following words reportedly said by Shaka: "Terror is the only thing Zulus understand, and you can rule Zulus only by killing them. Who are Zulus? They are unruly clans I had to break up and reshape, and only the fear of death will hold them together."

One evening Henry Fynn was watching Shaka and his Zulu warriors dance around the fire on the town square. Suddenly a man who was standing in the crowd of spectators rushed toward the dancers and stabbed Shaka with an assegai. He turned out to be an assassin from a rival tribe. Fynn was called to help treat Shaka's wound, which was not serious. Shaka, however, was convinced he was going to die. Panicked Zulus started gathering to mourn their chief. "Immense crowds of people were constantly arriving... they were shouting, throwing themselves on the ground... Many fainted from overexertion and excessive heat...Then they started killing one another. Some were put to death because they did not cry, others – for sitting down while crying..." Shaka's warriors found 3 men they suspected of being the assassin. They killed all three just in case. Shaka quickly recovered.

In 1827, when Shaka was 40 years old, Nandi, his mom and best friend, passed away. Shaka seemed to lose his mind from grief. His behavior was getting crazier and crazier. He executed about 7000 of his own people who, he claimed, were not crying hard enough at Nandi's funeral and during the 'year of mourning' that followed. He also prohibited planting crops or making milk products during that year. If any woman got pregnant during the 'year of mourning,' she was to be executed along with her husband.

On Shaka's orders, thousands of cows were slaughtered – supposedly to teach their calves what it meant to lose a mother... By this time Shaka had made so many enemies, it was just a matter of time until someone settled scores with him. Indeed, he had only one year to live. Neither magic spells, nor terror and mass executions protected him. He had no kids, but he still had a few half-brothers...

When Shaka sent all of his troops north, to punish a rebellion, two of his half-brothers ambushed and killed him in his kraal. News of the king's death quickly spread. Among the Zulus who rushed to the site of the assassination, was Chief Sotobe, loyal to Shaka. He called on the growing crowd to kill the assassins. But one of the brothers, Dingane, reminded them about Shaka's insane cruelty toward his own people, and the crowd fell silent. After an uncomfortable moment of hesitation, to everyone's surprise, Chief Sotobe suddenly admitted that he, too, had thoughts of killing Shaka. And so, Shaka's body was wrapped in a cowhide, tossed in an abandoned grain storage pit and covered with stones. Dingane became king of the Zulus.

Photos of Zulu families, 1912

MENELIK and TAYTU BETUL
1844 – 1913   1851 – 1918

In 1870 only 10% of Africa was controlled by the Europeans – mainly the areas around slave trading ports. In the 1880s slave labor started being replaced by agricultural machines, so slave trading shrank. At that point Europeans began to focus on the vast natural resources of the African continent – diamonds, gold, and, eventually rubber needed for the emerging car industry. The colonizing frenzy known as the **Scramble for Africa** started: Britain, France, Germany, Italy, Belgium, Spain, and Portugal carved up the continent, leaving only 2 countries independent – Liberia which had been created to resettle former African slaves from the United States back to Africa, and Ethiopia.

"I'll be seeing you!"

An ancient name for Ethiopia was Abyssinia. The word Abyssinia could come from the Amharic (Ethiopian) root 'hbsh' meaning mixed.' It may have pointed to the fact that Ethiopia was inhabited by different ethnic and racial groups. In the 1920-30s the word "Abyssinia" became a popular joke in English – a funny way to say 'goodbye' because it sounds like "I'll be seeing you!"

At the time of Menelik's birth in 1844, Ethiopia consisted of a number of kingdoms and princedoms. Menelik's father ruled one of them – the Kingdom of Shewa. There was also the emperor, Tewodros II, who was supposed to reign over all of Ethiopia, but most Ethiopian kings and warlords ignored him. Emperor Tewodros was seen as a merciful monarch (even though he was known for executing messengers who brought him bad news!).

Ethiopia was Christian, and its rulers disapproved of slavery and of the slave trading practiced by their Muslim neighbors. Tewodros banned the slave trade in the lands he controlled. However, he waged endless wars on rebellious provinces of his own country, and was ruthless toward rebels.

> ### Coffee
>
> *The English word 'coffee' comes from the Arabic 'qahwah,' which in turn comes from Kaffa – the name of a region in the southwestern highlands of Ethiopia, the native habitat of the coffee tree – Coffea arabica.*

When Menelik was 11, Emperor Tewodros decided to teach a lesson to Menelik's dad, the rebellious King of Shewa, and invaded his kingdom. The troops of Shewa were defeated, and Menelik's father died – of sickness, or of heartbreak. Menelik was captured and dragged in front of Emperor Tewodros. When they put chains on him, young Menelik, who had shown no fear until that moment, suddenly burst into tears. Emperor Tewodros was so moved by this, that he ordered Menelik released and adopted him as one of his own kids. Menelik lived at Tewodros' court, and traveled with him to Ethiopian army camps, receiving education and military training. When he grew up, he married one of the Emperor's daughters. But a year after the wedding, in 1865, Shewa rebelled again, and the rebellion leaders arranged an escape for Menelik and his mother. When Emperor Tewodros heard of Menelik's escape, he felt betrayed. "I don't blame him for escaping," he said, "but why did he leave his wife behind?"

Back in the Kingdom of Shewa, 21 year-old Menelik became king. In the very first days at his new court he met a woman with whom he fell in love. Her name was Bafena. His advisors told him that to marry this woman would be a very bad idea. Bafena was 10 years older than Menelik and had 8 sons and daughters by a whole bunch of husbands. "She will just use you to enrich her kids," Menelik's advisors told him. "She has no loyalty to you. Her loyalty is to her kids." But Menelik didn't listen. He divorced the emperor's daughter and married Bafena. Even though their marriage wasn't a church wedding, but a traditional ceremony following unwritten tribal traditions, Menelik demanded that his wife be treated as a queen.

Most of his advisors resigned rather than address Bafena as "Your Majesty." Menelik took away their lands and gave them to Bafena. Her sons were given titles and precious gifts.

Tewodros II

In 1868, three years after Menelik's escape, Emperor Tewodros got into trouble with the British. He had thrown in jail a British consul who could not explain why a letter Tewodros had written to Queen Victoria had not been answered. The British demanded his release, but Tewodros responded by taking 60 more Brits hostage! The consul begged Queen Victoria to answer the emperor's letter, but it looked like Tewodros' letter had been lost at the Foreign Office in London. Tewodros started drinking heavily and was acting crazy. Eventually, a British colonial army from India – 32,000 men, 44 elephants, and 176 Chinese *coolies* (workers) invaded Ethiopia. The coolies were supposed to build a supply railroad from the port of Zula inland – to support the invasion. The Brits meant business. Menelik received from them a message he couldn't read because he didn't know English. The Catholic priest who delivered the message translated it for him into **Amharic**, the Ethiopian language. The invaders were threatening Menelik with a quick defeat if he dared to help Tewodros. Soon the emperor's army was indeed slaughtered by the British forces, and the emperor committed suicide with a gun he had once received as a gift from Queen Victoria. Menelik encouraged his people to celebrate the death of the "evil Tewodros" who was hated in Shewa, but later he admitted that he, himself, wanted "to go into a forest and cry" over the death of the man who was a father figure to him.

As abruptly as they showed up, the British left Ethiopia, and in 1871 the throne of the Emperor of Ethiopia was seized by an Ethiopian warlord who took the name of Yohannes IV. Yohannes ruled Ethiopia for 18 years, but Menelik and other Ethiopian kings and princes ignored him, just as they had ignored Tewodros. Meanwhile a dark cloud was gathering over Menelik. His wife Bafena – just as Menelik's advisors had predicted – was plotting to secure the throne of Shewa for one of her sons. Menelik and Bafena didn't have kids, so her original plan was to convince the king to adopt one of her sons and make him the heir to the throne.

Coolies

'Coolies' were unskilled laborers from China – the cheapest work force in British colonies. The word 'coolie' comes from the Hindu 'kuli' – 'wages.' In the 19th century, as Chinese workers were brought to the Americas through the British colonies, the word 'coolie' became common in the US.

Bafena didn't feel she owed Menelik any loyalty. After all, during the 12 years they were together Menelik kept dating other women and had a few kids with his 'girlfriends.' Behind Menelik's back, Bafena got in touch with Emperor Yohannes, and convinced him to name her son the king of Shewa when the time comes. Bafena worked tirelessly to get rid of any potential rivals to her boy. She accused one of Menelik's cousins of treason. Menelik locked him up in jail at the cost of losing the support of the cousin's clan. Then, in 1877, when Menelik was away on a military campaign, Bafena released Menelik's cousin from jail, and convinced him to overthrow Menelik. But neither Menelik, nor his cousin wanted to fight with each other. They made peace, Bafena's conspiracy failed, and she was exiled to a remote village.

Taytu Betul

Menelik's third wife, Taytu Betul, was a princess from one of the Ethiopian royal families. The meaning of her name – Taytu – in the Amharic language is 'the Sun.' Before her marriage to Menelik, Taytu had been married 4 times! It wasn't unusual in Ethiopia, where royal marriages were used to seal alliances between kingdoms, clans, and tribes. If a marriage wasn't a 'church marriage,' divorce was permitted and not considered a big deal. However Taytu's wedding to Menelik was held at a church service on Easter Sunday in 1883. It was an *indissoluble* marriage – with no divorce permitted. Taytu was well-educated. She could read and write in two Ethiopian languages – Amharic and Ge'ez, composed poetry, took classes in law and theology, and was famous for her skill at chess. As Menelik's kingdom grew, Taytu became the head of his government. She was known for making quick decisions and standing her ground. Courtiers joked that her favorite expression was "Absolutely not," while Menelik's was "Yes, but not now." Taytu never had kids, probably due to a health condition. In Ethiopia childlessness was a valid reason for divorce, but Menelik didn't hold it against her. He recognized three of the 'illegitimate' children he had with his girlfriends as 'legitimate' and that took care of it.

One day, in 1887, after a feast, Menelik's court traveled to a valley famous for its hot springs and flowering mimosa trees. Taytu liked it so much, she gave the valley the name of Addis Ababa – "the new flower" and built a house there.

Immediately Menelik's generals and court ladies bought all the land around the royal house, and soon Addis Ababa turned into the capital of Shewa. Today it's the capital of Ethiopia.

Two years later, in 1889, Emperor Yohannes IV perished in a war against Egypt. Dying, he named one of his sons the heir to the Ethiopian crown, but Menelik rejected his wish. He was quoted saying, "God will give me the throne to which I had right all these years." Ethiopian royalty believed that their ancestors were King Solomon of Israel whose reign is described in the Old Testament of the Bible and Queen of Sheba who – according to Ethiopian legends – was Ethiopian. However, Menelik pointed out that Yohannes traced his family line to Solomon and Sheba following the female line – from mother to daughter, while he, Menelik, was their descendant based on the male line – from father to son. That made his claim far more valid in the eyes of Ethiopian nobles, and Menelik was crowned the Emperor.

1889 was the year Italy targeted Ethiopia as its potential colony. Fearing expansion of the French colonial power in Somaliland, the British encouraged Italy to take over neighboring Ethiopia. The Italians started their quest by occupying the coast of the Red Sea. They named their new colony ***Eritrea***. Menelik agreed to recognize Eritrea as the Italian colony in exchange for a bank loan and thousands of Remington rifles for his troops. To seal this understanding, the Ethiopians and Italians signed the Treaty of Wuchale. But the Italians cheated!
The Ethiopian, Amharic-language version of Article 17 of the Treaty of Wuchale said that Ethiopia "might use" the help of Italy in foreign affairs. But the Italian version said that Italy was to take over the entirety of the Ethiopian foreign policy and make all decisions for Ethiopia – which would have turned Ethiopia into an Italian ***protectorate***.

Eritrea

'Eritrea' comes from the Latin Mare Erythraeum, the Roman name for the Red Sea. Erythraeum was borrowed from Greek: 'erythros' = red. 'Ryth' in 'erythros' is the same root as the English word 'red.' Both languages inherited this root – independently – from ancient Indo-European languages.

Protectorate

A protectorate is a country that gives up its independence in exchange for military 'protection' by a more powerful country. Protectorates keep their own governments, but pay for the 'protection', either with their natural resources, or by hosting their protector's military bases, or by providing their troops to fight their protector's wars.

Italian governor of Eritrea General Baratieri

An Ethiopian biographer of Taytu described the following scene at the royal court. "A man from Eritrea learned that the Italians were saying that Ethiopia was now a protectorate of Italy. He rushed to the palace of Emperor Menelik to report this. Menelik was in the middle of a banquet. The man was in such a rush, he forgot to take off his shoes. Everyone was shocked, but Empress Taytu took him aside, listened to what he had to say, then turned to her husband and the guests and said, 'Will all the men rise? We are going to war against Italy.' Everyone stood up except her brother Wele. So Taytu said to him, 'Here, you take my skirt and I will wear your pants.'"

Italian diplomats at Menelik's court viewed Africans as naive and corrupt. Unaware that Menelik was on the verge of rejecting the treaty, they tried another trick on him. The Italian negotiator informed Menelik that Italy would raise its flag in Aussa, in eastern Ethiopia, because that "would prevent the British and the French from invading that region." In his report the Italian diplomat said he had to stop talking about the flag abruptly because "the empress rose up in anger," and Menelik closed the conversation with, "Aussa is mine."

Italian diplomats also pressed Menelik to come up with an official agreement in which he would confirm Article 17 of the Treaty of Wuchale, and they thought they were succeeding. "Menelik says he will certainly call upon Italy for help in foreign affairs, not through force, but because of friendship," wrote one of the Italian negotiators in his diary. So the agreement was prepared – in Amharic. The Italian chief negotiator Count Antonelli glanced over it with his interpreter and signed it. That evening, as the interpreter started working on the official Italian translation of the agreement, he spotted in it an Amharic word he didn't know and couldn't find in the dictionary. He asked around, and, to his horror, learned that the meaning of the word was 'to cancel.' The Italians signed a document canceling Article 17! Antonelli rushed to Menelik's palace. He loudly protested and tore up the agreement, trying not to look at Taytu who was openly laughing at him. "It's a mistake made by the interpreter!" he complained. Suddenly Taytu stood up: "And whose mistake is this?" She held out the Amharic version of Article 17. "Show me here the words that give Italy the right to make decisions for Ethiopia," she said. Antonelli fell silent. Those words existed only in the Italian translation of Article 17.

When Menelik rejected the treaty with Italy, Italians first tried to bribe him with 2 million rounds of ammunition for the Remington rifles, and when Menelik refused to negotiate, they attempted to provoke a civil war in Ethiopia. That scheme also failed. So both sides started preparing for war.

The Ethiopians, however, faced a serious challenge. To feed their army, the Italians brought cows from India. The cows happened to be infected with parasites that quickly spread around Ethiopia killing thousands of cattle. Ethiopia was struck by a multi-year famine. General Baratieri, commander of the Italian forces in Eritrea, was convinced that the famine and constant infighting between Ethiopian warlords would prevent Menelik from raising a big enough army that could pose a real threat to the Italians. "The internal and external situation is tranquil," he reported. Meanwhile Menelik's army already numbered 100 thousand men armed with rifles and artillery that were far better and more modern than the weapons of the Italians.

In October 1895 Menelik and Taytu left Addis Ababa, leading their army to face the enemy.

The Battle for the Italian fort of Amba Alagi was the first clash between Ethiopians and Italians. Ethiopia lost 500 soldiers, but the Italian garrison of over 2000 was almost entirely wiped out.

Ethiopian commander Ras Makonnen at Amba Alagi; Left: Siege of Amba Alagi

More battles followed, more forts were taken by Menelik's army. General Baratieri, under pressure from the Italian government to "save the honor of the army and the prestige of the Italian monarchy," was drunk almost every night and made blunder after blunder. The decisive battle of the war was the Battle of Adwa. The Italian troops suffered a humiliating defeat. Large numbers of them were taken prisoner. Those who failed to run away tried to hide among the dead, waiting for the night. Seeing this tactic, the Ethiopians set the grass on fire, forcing the enemy from hiding. Italian prisoners were spared, but the Eritreans who fought on the Italian side were punished – each one had their right hand and left foot cut off. When the Europeans called this "barbarism," the Ethiopians pointed out that the Eritreans weren't Italians, they were Ethiopian traitors, and in Europe the punishment for treason was death.

During the battle, Empress Taytu commanded her own force of 5000 men – and hundreds of women whose job was to carry water from the river to Menilek's troops, and take care of the wounded. After the Battle of Adwa Taytu's pictures appeared in all European newspapers. She became a celebrity – a "warrior queen." An article in the British *Spectator* magazine concluded: "The Italians have suffered a great disaster ... greater than has ever occurred in modern times to white men in Africa." Indeed, it was the second great victory of native Africans against the European colonial powers after the victory of the Zulus over the British in the battle of Isandlwana in 1879. After the Battle of Adwa Italians expected Menelik to march into Eritrea, but Menelik stopped his troops. He knew that the Italians would come back with a bigger force and make more war, so he proposed that Italy keep Eritrea and leave the rest of Ethiopia alone. The Italians agreed and signed the Treaty of Addis Ababa recognizing Ethiopian independence. Emperor Menelik II died in 1913, and his daughter Zewditu became the Empress of Ethiopia.

Ethiopian military commanders wearing lion-mane crowns

Yaa Asantewaa
1840 – 1921

Yaa Asantewaa was the Queen Mother of Ejisu – a region within the Ashanti (or Asante) Empire that flourished on the territory of modern-day Ghana from the 17th to the 20th century. The Ashanti Empire united many tribes ruled by local kings under one leader. The Ashanti lands were rich in gold, so the symbol of Ashanti unity and the most sacred object in the Empire was the so-called Golden Stool – a traditional seat of a tribal chief made of solid gold. The Ashanti believed that the soul of their nation lived inside the Golden Stool.

In the 15th century the Ashanti experienced their first contact with Europeans when they started trading with the Portuguese, selling gold and slaves. In 1752, the British established the Gold Coast colony on the Gulf of Guinea. They were buying slaves, gold, diamonds, wood, ivory, and cocoa from the Ashanti. By the 1820s they decided to push the borders of their colony inland, into the Ashanti lands. This resulted in three Anglo-Ashanti wars.

The first, the 1824 Anglo-Ashanti war, ended in a crushing defeat of the British forces led by the military governor of the West African Gold Coast, General MacCarthy. Arrogant and ignorant about Africa, MacCarthy reported to London that the Ashanti were unskilled and "unprepared for war." He was so wrong. Ashanti troops were the only native African army that fought in formations, was armed with muskets, and "marched in perfect order, their guns carried at exactly the same angle, before they turned toward the enemy and fired on command" (from the book *Arrogant Armies: Great Military Disasters and the Generals Behind Them* by James Perry). The Ashanti didn't always have ammunition for the muskets, but they came up with a highly-creative solution, replacing bullets with nails that killed just as well.

A 20-cedis bill (Ghana) featuring Yaa Asantewaa

In the very first battle against the Ashanti army, British troops ran out of ammunition and were destroyed. General MacCarthy was killed, and his skull was turned into a gold-rimmed drinking cup for the Ashanti rulers.

The Second Anglo-Ashanti war resulted in a treaty that didn't last long. By the third war, the British had learned their lesson. This time they were prepared. They cut down the trees around the 160-mile (260km) road that led inland, from the Gold Coast to Kumasi, the capital of the Ashanti Empire. The road was widened to move British troops and artillery more easily. They laid telegraph cable and built a fort every 10 miles. They built 237 bridges! The British force brought to fight the Ashanti was massive. Along with the British soldiers, it included two 'West India Regiments' recruited from amongst former West African slaves in the Caribbean. The British ran the Ashanti out of their capital, burned Kumasi and demolished the royal palace with explosives. The Ashanti king signed a treaty promising to pay the British an *indemnity* (compensation for the war), 50 thousand ounces of gold, to allow free trade between the Ashanti and the British, and to forever ban human sacrifice from Ashanti religious rituals.

The Fourth Anglo-Ashanti war occurred in 1895. The British pressed the 28-year-old Ashanti king Prempeh I to sign an agreement declaring the Ashanti tribal lands to be a British protectorate.

A still from the 1914 British silent movie 'Sixty Years a Queen': Queen Victoria listens to a report about the colonization of Africa; Right: A stool of an Ashanti chief and the Golden Stool of the Ashanti Empire

Prempeh refused. He also refused to pay the indemnity – the cost of the 1874 British military expedition to defeat the Ashanti. So the British invaded the Ashanti Empire again and captured King Prempeh. To humiliate the king, British Governor Maxwell demanded that the king perform the native Ashanti ritual of submission. The king and the Queen Mother kneeled in front of the governor and embraced his legs. After that the king and other royals were imprisoned in the Seychelles (islands in the Indian Ocean far away on the other side of Africa). The Ashanti lands became the protectorate of Great Britain. One of the British colonial commanders, Robert Baden-Powell, in his diary, gave these reasons for the invasion: 1. King Prempeh failed to pay the indemnity; 2. The Ashanti never outlawed human sacrifice; 3. The Ashanti continued trading in slaves, which was by that time banned in both Europe and the United States. However, the real reason for the invasion was entirely different. It was to prevent the French and the Germans from seizing the Ashanti gold.

The founder of the Boy Scouts movement

Lord Robert Baden-Powell fought in a number of the colonial wars that expanded the British Empire. He fought in Afghanistan and South Africa in addition to the African Gold Coast. Having retired from his military career, Baden-Powell did something quite wonderful – he created the Boy Scout and Girl Scout movement. Robert Baden-Powell was viewed as a military hero, and was a role model for young people throughout his life. But as the anti-colonial movement uncovered the many crimes committed by the British colonial troops, he became a controversial figure. For example, his critics recall that during the Second Matabele War in South Africa Baden-Powell was accused of executing a rebellious Matabele chief who surrendered after being promised his life if he would lay down his arms. To justify his actions Baden-Powell said the chief was badly wounded and was unlikely to survive the journey to face the British colonial court, so he ordered him shot. The British military court accepted this explanation and let Baden-Powel go. In 1908 Baden-Powell published his famous book **Scouting for Boys**. *He developed his ideas for kids' outdoors activities based on the techniques of military scouting (reconnaissance / spying) and also on the survival methods of native African tribes, such as the Zulus and Matabele, against whom he led the colonizing British troops.*

Below: Robert Baden-Powell; the burning of Kumasi;
Right: The humiliation of King Prempeh

For centuries the Ashanti had kept the location of their gold mines a secret. Another secret was the fact that most of their gold didn't come from the mines. They got it by panning the sand from riverbeds rich in gold-bearing quartz rocks. But in the 1870s a Frenchman who had been a prisoner in one of the Ashanti tribes brought the legends of the Ashanti gold to Europe, and a gold rush began. The Ashanti opened some of their mines to the Europeans, but this only increased the colonial powers' interest in seizing the Ashanti lands.

Panning Gold

"Panning" is using a bowl to scoop up water and sand from the river and twirl the contents of the bowl so that the lighter materials wash out over the rim. Gold is heavier than sand, so it stays in the bowl – while the sand is washed away.

The Ashanti understood that the war was about their gold. So it's not surprising that the Fifth Anglo-Ashanti war was named "The War of the Golden Stool." The Ashanti forces were led by a 60-year-old grandmother, Yaa Asantewaa, the Queen Mother of the Ejisu, and the guardian of the Golden Stool. Her grandson was one of the Ashanti princes imprisoned by the British in the Seychelles along with King Prempeh.

Why didn't the Ashanti stop the slave trade?

In 1807 the British prohibited the slave trade and stopped buying slaves in Africa. But for the Ashanti the end of the slave trade was a problem. First of all they were puzzled by the fact that for 300 years it had been OK to buy and sell slaves, and then, suddenly, it became "wrong" and illegal. After centuries of growing their empire, the Ashanti had a huge army. It kept conquering new lands and putting down riots among the defeated tribes. Enemy warriors and leaders were routinely sold as slaves to Arab and European slave traders – never to return to Africa. The money (gold and cowrie shells) made on slave sales helped feed and arm Ashanti warriors. So even when the British outlawed the slave trade, the Ashanti kept sellling slaves to other 'customers,' such as Arab slave traders.

In 1900 a new British governor, Frederick Hodgson, arrived in Kumasi. Here is a passage from a memoir, *The Ashanti Campaign of 1900*, published in London by two officers who served in the British colonial troops, Captain Armitage and Lieutenant-Colonel Montanaro. The authors describe the arrival of Governor Hodgson:

The Gold regalia of Ashanti kings looted by the British colonial troops and kept at the British Museum in London

"At 4 P.M. the fort bugles announced His Excellency. The guard of honour presented arms, and the Governor, dressed in full uniform, and accompanied by Lady Hodgson, took his seat and received each Ashanti king in turn, shaking hands with them. The old Queen Mother of Ejisu, Yaa Asantewaa, whose name has since figured so largely in the rebellion, caused much amusement by carefully examining the Governor's medals. On the completion of this ceremony, the Governor addressed the assembly... He informed the kings that the time had now come to do something towards paying off the war indemnity...This announcement was received in silence..." And then Governor Hodgson opened his mouth again, and out of it came something that shocked the Ashanti chiefs and motivated them to rise against the British. According to Armitage and Montanaro, "The Governor proceeded to ask where the Golden Stool was, and why it had not been given up to him, as the representative of the Great White Queen [Queen Victoria]. Although the Ashantis might keep the Stool, we, he said, still have the power."

Enraged by the arrogance of the governor and the demand for the Golden Stool, the symbol of the Ashanti nation, the Ashanti chiefs hid the Stool and called a secret war council. When some chiefs suggested that it was useless to resist the British, Yaa Asantewaa said, "You don't want to fight? Then I'll call on women. We will fight the white men until the last of us falls in the battlefields!" To conclude her speech, she grabbed a gun and fired a shot in the air.

A couple days later Captain Armitage left Kumasi with a unit of the British soldiers. His task was to find the Golden Stool. "A boy, who had promised to guide us to the spot where the Golden Stool and Prempeh's treasures were hidden accompanied me," he wrote. They arrived in a remote Ashanti village. "Here, according to our guide, under the flooring of the huts, lay the Golden Stool and Prempeh's treasure. The picks and shovels we had brought with us were at once produced, and every one laboured amid great excitement to dig up the floor of the largest hut." But soon "excitement gave way to disappointment, for there was no sign of buried treasure."

The great war drum of the Ashanti in the royal palace at Kumasi. The skulls belonged to the chiefs of defeated tribes.

During this treasure-hunting expedition, Armitage realized that in every village they passed, the Ashanti were preparing for war. Armitage quotes the words of a war song the Ashanti were singing: "The Governor came up to Kumasi, demanded money from us and sent white men to bring him the Golden Stool. Instead of money the Governor shall have the white men's heads sent to him. The Golden Stool shall be well washed in the white man's blood."

Governor Hodgson telegraphed the British forts on the coast, calling for reinforcements. But the Ashanti cut the telegraph wire. The rebels sent 5 conditions on which they were prepared to negotiate peace. "The Ashanti terms, five in number, are so weird that I quote them in full," wrote Captain Armitage.

1. The Ashantis will be in future excused from carrying loads or building houses for the British.
2. Slavery to be allowed.
3. All traders from the coast will leave the Ashanti land.
4. The white men will return to the coast and won't trouble the Ashantis further.
5. The British Fort in Kumasi will be destroyed.

Armitage continued, "Our messengers returned to the rebel camp to inform the chiefs that far from them dictating terms to the white man, it was for the chiefs to accept the white man's terms before the white man's soldiers carry fire and sword through the Ashanti land."

The negotiations failed and within a month the 5000-strong Ashanti army led by Yaa Asantewa surrounded Kumasi. The siege began.

Above: "The siege of Kumasi, Governor Hodgson" by Richard Caton Woodville
Left: "The Ashanti Ambush" by Arthur Hopkins

After 2 months with hardly any food and ammunition left, the governor escaped to the coast with a few officers and gathered an army of 1,400 troops from across the many British colonies in Africa to fight Yaa Asantewa's rebels – who now numbered 50 thousand warriors. However, the Ashanti didn't have modern weapons, and after a 3-month war, despite their overwhelming numbers, they were defeated. Yaa Asantewa was captured and sent to Seychelles where she died in 1921.

The same year, native workers building a road in one of the Ashanti tribal lands found two large brass containers in which the Golden Stool had been buried. Ashanti elders rushed to the spot and scared away the workers by telling them that the brass boxes contained smallpox. They dug out the stool and placed it in one of their homes. There the stool was discovered by a couple of curious Ashanti teenagers who had no idea what a sacred object it was. They tore some gold ornaments off it and headed to the market to sell them. An Ashanti grandma who remembered seeing the stool back in 1896 spotted the gold and the kids were forced to return it.

In 1924, the British allowed King Prempeh to return to West Africa and rule while recognizing that Ashantiland was now a colony of the British Empire. In 1935 the British granted the Ashanti self-rule and the Golden Stool was shown in public for the first time since 1896 at the coronation ceremony of King Prempeh II. In 1957 the Ashanti kingdom became part of Ghana, the first country in Sub-Saharan Africa to gain independence.

Yaa Asantewaa monument in Ejisu, Ghana; King Prempeh in 1922

Kente cloth

Hand-woven Kente cloth was worn for centuries by Ashanti royalty. It's one of the most recognizable traditional African fabric designs, still manufactured and worn in Ghana. Kente cloth has become a symbol of African identity.

HAILE SELASSIE
1892 – 1975

In 1930 Empress Zewditu of Ethiopia, daughter of Menelik II, passed away. She had no kids, so Ethiopian prince Ras Tafari, a great grandson of Ethiopian King Sahle Selassie, was crowned emperor under the name Haile Selassie. His dad, Ras Makonnen, was one of Emperor Menelik's military commanders who defeated the Italian colonial troops in the Battle of Adwa. In Ge'ez, one of the languages of Ethiopia, Haile Selassie's name means 'The Power of the Trinity.'

Haile Selassie's rise to the Ethiopian throne was not entirely peaceful. In 1916 24-year-old Haile Selassie was appointed the Crown Prince of Ethiopia. He was popular both at the court and with common Ethiopians. In the book *Haile Selassie, Emperor of Ethiopia* written in 1935, five years into his rule, his biographer, Ethiopian Princess Asfa Yilma, writes: "He won all hearts by his simplicity, his natural easy-going manners, and above all by his gift for all kinds of sport. Because to a man who is outstanding in sport, whether it is running, riding, shooting or the throwing of the spear, the Abyssinians give a whole-hearted hero-worship."

In the following years Haile Selassie's influence on the Ethiopian government grew until he became the ***de facto*** Ethiopian ruler. But Haile Selassie's vision for the future of his country clashed with that of Empress Zewditu.

Empress Zewditu

Latin: De Facto and De Jure

Expressions De Facto and De Jure are legal (law) terms that come from Latin.
De Facto *= of the fact, 'done deed' – something that exists, that is real, whether or not it is allowed by law*
De Jure *= of the law – legitimate, lawful, allowed*

Haile Selassie's wife, Empress Menen Asfaw

Empress Zewditu was against any modernization of Ethiopia, against any dealing with the European powers, against introducing European-style education and even book printing because, as an Ethiopian bishop, who was close to the court, said, "If you have too many books they will become so common that no one will consider as wisdom what is to be found within their covers." But Haile Selassie traveled across Europe, wanted to adopt a constitution, and planned to introduce reforms that would make Ethiopia more like a European monarchy. In 1923 Ethiopia became a member of the ***League of Nations***. As a condition for joining the League of Nations, Haile Selassie abolished slavery.

It wasn't an easy task. Emperor Menelik II tried to ban it, and as did other emperors and kings before him, but Ethiopian chiefs and warlords typically ignored orders from Addis Ababa. In the 1920s there were still over 2 million slaves in Ethiopia.

And there was yet another problem. Empress Zewditu couldn't stand Haile Selassie's wife, Menen Asfaw. Haile Selassie and Menen Asfaw had six kids. 5 of them were born during the reign of Empress Zewditu, and court gossipers were convinced the childless empress was bitterly envious of Menen Asfaw's happy marriage.

Empress Zewditu was married four times. Her marriages were all arranged by her dad, Menelik II, as a way to seal strategic agreements with warlords who supported him. None of them lasted. As soon as each agreement lost political importance, Zewditu's husbands divorced her. Princess Asfa Yilma also blamed Zewditu herself. Her father Menelik was such a hero to her, she writes, that Zewditu viewed other men, including her husbands, as "poor specimens at best" – not good enough. "The unhappiness which she experienced in her marriages undoubtedly poisoned her life and made her very difficult to deal with."

The League of Nations

The League of Nations was an organization similar to the United Nations. It was founded in 1920 after the First World War. Its goal was to promote peace and prevent another world-wide conflict. The organization was not successful. Germany, Italy, and Japan left the League to create a Hitler-led alliance. The United States never joined it, and the Soviet Union was kicked out of it in 1939 for invading Finland, which, it claimed, was another ally of Hitler.

Haile Selassie and his court; Haile Selassie and his pet cheetahs

In 1930, Empress Zewditu's ex-husband, Ethiopian army commander Gugsa Welle, organized a rebellion against Haile Selassie's government, but was defeated and killed in battle. Two days after his death Empress Zewditu died. Some historians believe she died of shock and grief over his defeat and death. Others say she had a really bad fever and took a bath of ice water that made her condition worse and killed her.

Here is how Princess Asfa Yilma described the daily life of the Emperor Haile Selassie: "Between the hours of four and five in the morning his personal servant comes to wake him up and often finds the Emperor already awake and in prayer. Having prayed, he goes to his study where the Ministers of State bring news and reports from the governments of provinces connected to the capital by telegraph; there are also messages brought by runners from more isolated districts...The orders for the day are given. There is now a break while the Emperor drinks coffee, eats bread and fruit and glances at the latest issue of his newspaper *Light and Peace*, for which he often writes articles... The advertisements in the paper feature gramophones, soaps, medicines, and luxuries from France..."

"...One of the sights which surprise the visitors to the royal palace are the lions that live there. Often the Emperor strolls in his gardens accompanied by two playful lion cubs." The princess recalls that one day an English official visiting the royal palace found 2 lions sitting at the door of Haile Selassie's study. "He thought it was a bad joke and shot them both with his revolver! Actually he was not in any danger, though it may well be that it was intended to test his nerve."

"The custom of Ethiopia demands the exchange of gifts between hosts and guests, and between travelers who pass one another in the hills or deserts," continues the author of *Haile Selassie, Emperor of Ethiopia*. Once the emperor was told there was an engineer who came to the palace asking to see him, but "He has brought no gift!" Haile Selassie responded, "Good advice is better than any gift," and invited the engineer in. So many European government officials seeking business or favors arrived with lavish, crazily-expensive gifts, that at the royal court in Addis Ababa they made fun of them saying, "The size of the gift is a measure of the intended fraud."

Emperor Haile Selassie knew that even though Menelik II won Ethiopia its independence in the Battle of Adwa and sacrificed Eritrea to the Italians to buy peace for his country, that victory wasn't final. Italy wasn't satisfied. After the defeat of Germany in the First World War, the European powers divided the spoils. But Italy got hardly anything. All the German colonies in Africa went to England, France, and Belgium. In the 1930s Italy was led by the *fascist* government of Benito Mussolini. The fascists viewed the Italian defeat in the Battle of Adwa as a humiliation that must be avenged.

Left: Benito Mussolini; Italian troops
Below: Ethiopian troops

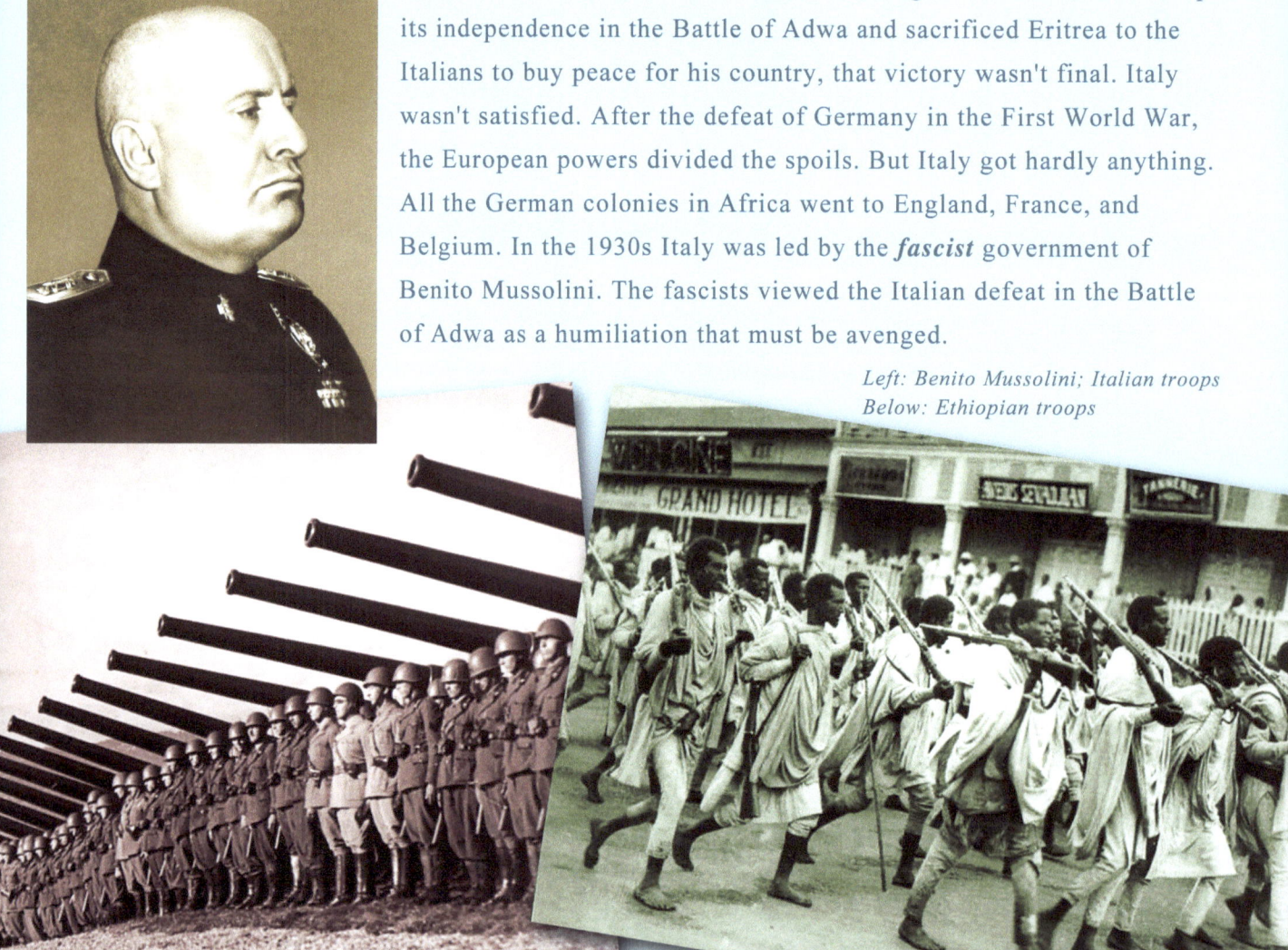

They also needed to distract the public from the disastrous state of the Italian economy, stuck in the Great Depression. Everyone knew another war was coming. Fearing that Mussolini would make friends with Hitler's Nazi Germany, British and French politicians tried to keep him happy. They didn't dare to protest the buildup of the Italian troops on the borders of Ethiopia.

So, in October of 1935, the Second Italo-Ethiopian War began. Two Italian armies invaded Ethiopia – one from Eritrea and one from Somalia (which was also a colony of Italy). Their soldiers were a mix of Italians and native Somalis and Eritreans. Mussolini believed that propaganda victories were as important as successes on the battlefield, so 200 Italian journalists accompanied the troops to report on the campaign and praise Mussolini's leadership.

Fascism

Fascism is an ideology promoting rule by a dictatorial leader, militarism, and aggressive nationalism. The word 'fascism' comes from the Latin fasces – a bundle of sticks carried before Roman magistrates (elected officials) as a symbol of power. Fascism first appeared in Italy before the Second World War, and spread to other countries in Europe.

Three days later Adwa – the place of Menelik's great triumph over the Italians – was captured. Next fell Aksum. The first thing the Italians did was topple down the famous 160-ton obelisk erected by King Ezana of Aksum in the 4th century. They cut it into 3 pieces and shipped it to Rome, where it was reassembled and put in front of the Ministry for Italian Africa. Haile Selassie ordered a total military mobilization of all Ethiopian men. Their wives were mobilized too – to cook for the troops. "Anyone found at home after receiving this order will be hanged."

Hitler at a parade of the German Nazi troops. Ezana of Axum's obelisk, stolen by the Italians in 1935, remained in Rome until 2008, when it was returned to Ethiopia.

Ethiopian troops counterattacked, but they were poorly armed and trained. Many mobilized men had spears and swords instead of guns, while Italians brought tanks and planes, and cutting-edge weaponry. Plus they were able to intercept Ethiopian radio communications and knew every detail of Haile Selassie's plans. Ethiopians lost battle after battle, and as their final defeat was nearing, Haile Selassie's troops retreated to Lake Ashenge in the south of Ethiopia. That's where Mussolini's commanders played their last deadly card – chemical weapons. Using special sprayers installed on dozens of planes, they covered the waters of the lake with poison gas – *mustard gas* and *phosgene*, killing thousands of Haile Selassie's troops. Ethiopians lost almost 9000 men, while the Italian casualties – both Europeans and Eritreans – were barely over a thousand. In addition Italians dispersed poison gas over vast areas of the Ethiopian countryside, killing thousands of civilians who ate crops or drank water in the sprayed areas.

In Addis Ababa, hearing the news of the defeat, angry locals started looting European shops. This turned into massive riots and fires that destroyed most of the city. Haile Selassie took a train to the neighboring country of Djibouti carrying with him the gold of the Ethiopian Central Bank. Italian commanders knew about this from radio intercepts and asked Mussolini to approve their plan to bomb the train, but Mussolini decided to let Haile Selassie go. From Djibouti Haile Selassie fled to England. King Victor Emmanuel III of Italy was proclaimed the Emperor of Ethiopia.

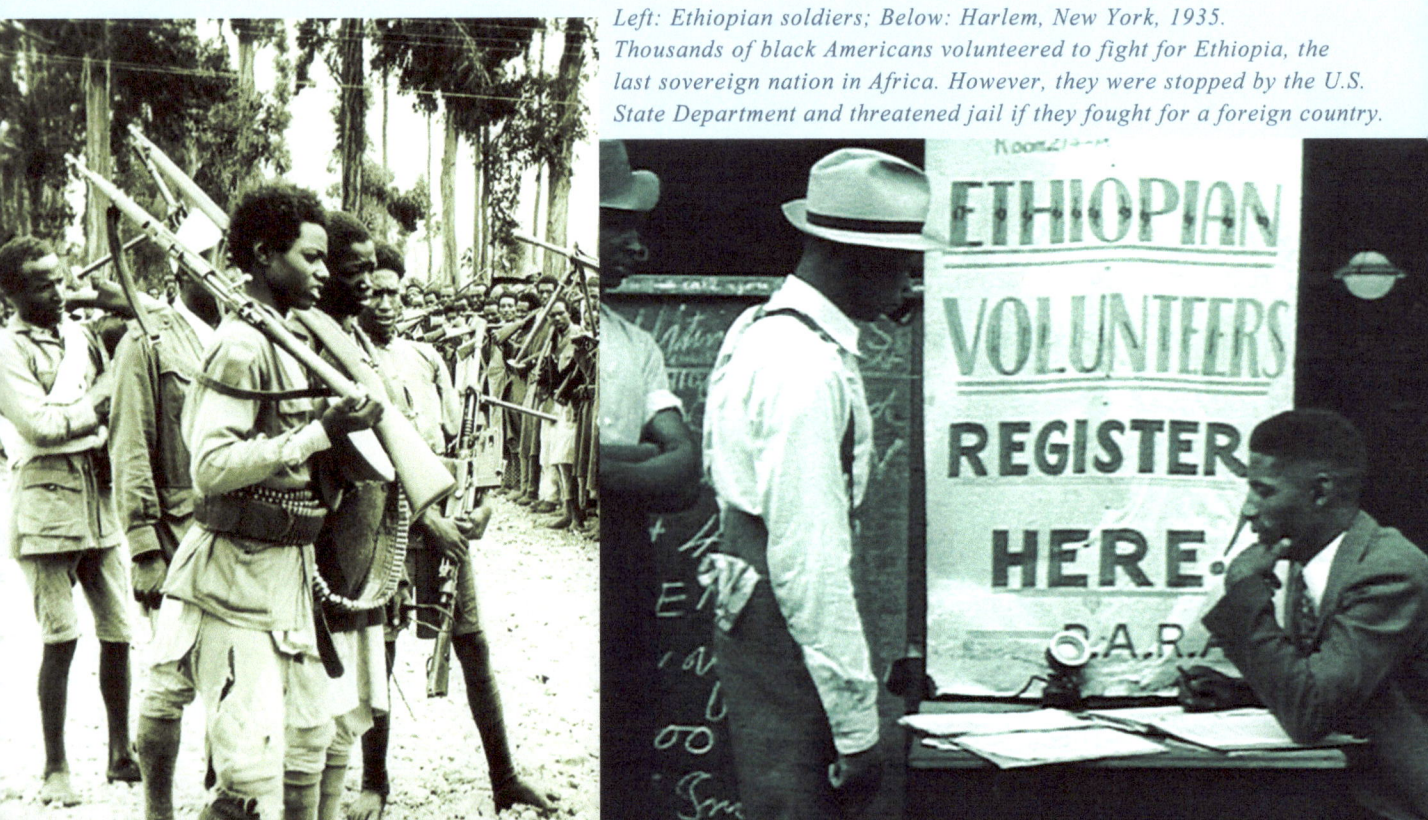

Left: Ethiopian soldiers; Below: Harlem, New York, 1935. Thousands of black Americans volunteered to fight for Ethiopia, the last sovereign nation in Africa. However, they were stopped by the U.S. State Department and threatened jail if they fought for a foreign country.

Most of the international community caved to Mussolini's bullying and agreed to view the Italian occupation of Ethiopia as legitimate. Only 6 countries in the world refused to recognize Ethiopia as an Italian colony: the United States, the Soviet Union, China, Mexico, Spain, and New Zealand. His success in Ethiopia encouraged Mussolini. Fascist Italy invaded Albania, and also signed a treaty of cooperation – the Pact of Steel – with Nazi Germany.

Ethiopians continued resistance using guerilla tactics – cutting telephone wires, blowing up Italian trucks, rolling giant boulders off cliffs onto the roads… but Mussolini was ruthless in suppressing them. In one rebel town Mussolini ordered the execution of every man over the age of 18. Guerillas taken prisoner were shot. Priests of the Ethiopian Orthodox Christian Church were hunted down and killed in revenge for each guerilla attack, because Mussolini suspected that the church encouraged the guerillas to fight for their country's sovereignty.
In 1938 a group of young Ethiopians from royal families tried to assassinate the Italian governor of Ethiopia. The plot failed, and, in revenge, Mussolini issued a secret order to execute all Ethiopians who held any government jobs. He believed they were all traitors, even if they worked for the Italian authorities. To prevent their escape, Italians told these Ethiopian officials that the King of Italy had invited them to visit Rome. So the Ethiopians boarded planes to Rome only to be thrown overboard once the aircraft took off. A new idiom appeared in the Ethiopian language – 'to go to Rome.' It meant 'to die.' Haile Selassie's two sons-in-law were executed by the Italians. One of his daughters, with her kids, was captured and imprisoned in Italy. She died there.

Italy must "initiate and systematically conduct a policy of terror and extermination against the rebels and the population in complicity with them," wrote Mussolini. "Without a policy of ten eyes to one, we cannot heal this wound in good time." Mussolini's goal was, to use his term, the "gradual liquidation" of the local population, with a plan to replace them with millions of Italian colonists. The Italians had already done this in Libya. There they had locked in concentration camps and executed hundreds of thousands of native people, as well as chased whole tribes away into neighboring countries.

In exile Haile Selassie appealed to the League of Nations, the US, and European countries for help, but they ignored him. The Second World War had begun, and all eyes were on Europe, not on Ethiopia. Only in 1940, when Italy attacked British colonial troops in Egypt, Sudan, Kenya, and Somaliland, did the British suddenly become interested in joining forces with the Ethiopian resistance fighters. Haile Selassie rushed to Sudan to make this happen.

Ethiopian camel troops; a 14-year-old Ethiopian volunteer soldier

The British-Ethiopian operations were so successful that a year later, in 1941, the resistance troops liberated Addis Ababa, and Haile Selassie returned to Ethiopia.

The post-war era became the era of the **Cold War** – the standoff between the two superpowers, the United States and the Soviet Union (the former Russian Empire). The world was defined as the West vs the East. The Soviet Union actively sided with anti-colonial native independence movements in Africa, while the United States and other Western countries usually supported the African 'puppet governments' that had been installed by their former colonial 'masters' – Britain, France, Belgium, and others. Haile Selassie took the side of the West, and that sealed the fate of the Ethiopian monarchy. The monarchy wasn't popular with the young educated Ethiopians, while Ethiopian farmers were ready to rebel because of the medieval laws that kept them in hopeless poverty. Only 7% of the Ethiopian farmland belonged to farmers. The rest belonged to the church (25%), the emperor (20%), aristocracy (30%), and the government (18%). In 1960 the officers of the Imperial Guard plotted to overthrow Haile Selassie, but failed. Soon, however, the rebels found a powerful ally: Haile Selassie made enemies in Moscow. He sent Ethiopian troops to support the Americans in the Korean War, fighting for South Korea – with the Soviet Union supporting the opposite side, North Korea. Haile Selassie also provided Ethiopian troops to the United Nations' peace-keeping force in Congo, where, instead of helping the government of the decolonized Congo, the 'peace keepers' guarded the interests of the US and European mining companies extracting uranium and other natural resources. This resulted in the overthrow and death of Patrice Lumumba, the first president of Congo, who was viewed as a hero in the Soviet Union. Moscow never forgave Haile Selassie for this.

In 1973 the biggest ever famine struck Ethiopia. Up to 80 thousand Ethiopians starved to death. Plus, oil prices went sky-high, crippling the Ethiopian economy. Government officials across Ethiopia tried to hide the massive scale of this tragedy, so it's not clear whether the 82-year-old Haile Selassie was fully aware of what was going on outside of his capital city. The anti-monarchy opposition blamed everything on the emperor. To encourage them, the Soviet Union unleashed a propaganda war against Haile Selassie, portraying him as an enemy of his own people. Liberal Ethiopian journalists, university professors, students – all supported this campaign. Ethiopian TV played non-stop a documentary where video footage of people dying of hunger alternated with scenes of feasts being enjoyed in the royal palace. A steady stream of money was secretly flowing to the rebels from the Soviet Union. Finally, a mutiny erupted in the Ethiopian army. Then students and farmers joined to launch an uprising. The army seized the emperor and placed him under house arrest in his palace. His family members were locked up in prison, and 60 of his top government officials were executed by firing squad without trial. Among them was one of Haile Selassie's grandchildren. Eventually, the rebels declared the end of the monarchy. Ethiopia became the People's Democratic Republic of Ethiopia.

About a year after the onset of the Ethiopian Revolution, the rebels announced that the emperor had died in his palace. It took 20 years for them to admit that Heile Selassie was strangled in his bed by army officers while under house arrest. The People's Democratic Republic of Ethiopia lasted until 1991 when the Soviet Union fell apart, and its heir, Russia, rejected communist ideology and stopped supporting the governments that were the 'puppets' of the Soviet Union.

Non-Aligned Countries and Collective Security

Haile Selassie wanted Ethiopia to be a non-aligned country – not an ally of either the United States or the Soviet Union, but he accepted the idea of 'collective security' promoted by the League of Nations and the United Nations. 'Collective security' means if one country is threatened, others join in defending it even if they are not under threat. Haile Selassie didn't see the obvious:
The superpowers used the 'collective security' idea to fight each other on other nations' soil. The Korean War (1950-53), the Vietnam War (1955-64), the Laos Civil War (1959-75), the Cambodian Civil War (1967-75), the Yom Kippur War between Israel and Arab nations (1973) and other conflicts were – in the end – wars between the United States and the Soviet Union who divided the world into their 'spheres of influence.'

Mengistu Haile Mariam, one of the leaders of the Ethiopian Revolution and the dictatorial head of state of Ethiopia (1977-1991), rumored to have murdered Haile Selassie

Rastafarianism

The word 'Rastafarian' comes from 'Ras Tafari,' where 'Ras' = head, chief, and 'Tafari' is the name of Haile Selassie before he became an emperor. Rastafarianism is a religion that emerged in Jamaica in the 1930s. It attributed to Haile Selassie the powers of a prophet, and some believers saw in him the reincarnation of Jesus Christ. Rastafarianism was not only a religion, but also a social movement focused on the liberation of Africa from colonialism, overcoming the legacy (consequences) of slavery in the Caribbean nations, and repatriation (returning) back to Africa. Rastas – the Rastafari believers – promote simple, close-to-nature lifestyle and wear their hair in dreadlocks.

The flag of the Ethiopian Empire; Rastas; Haile Selassie

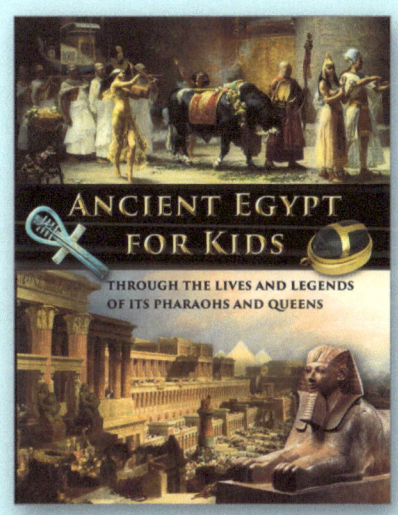
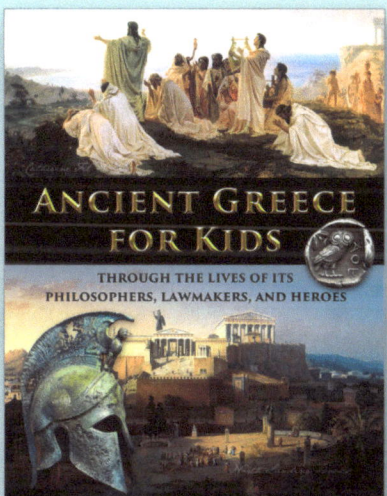
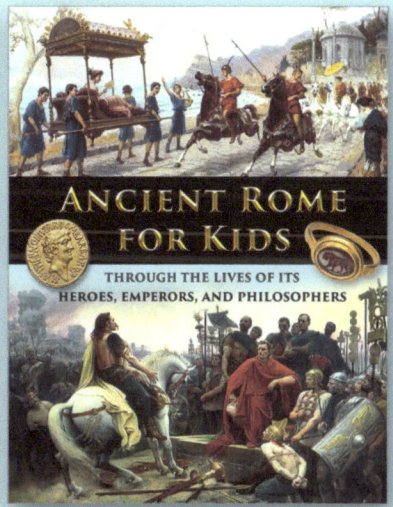
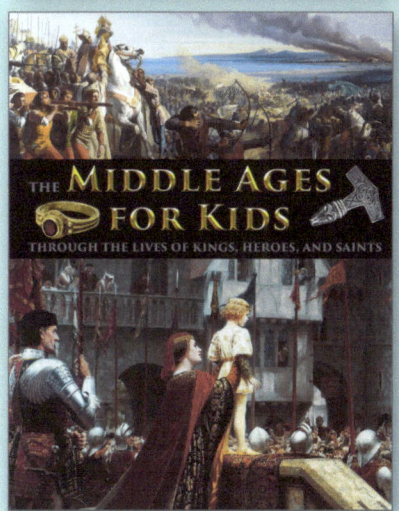
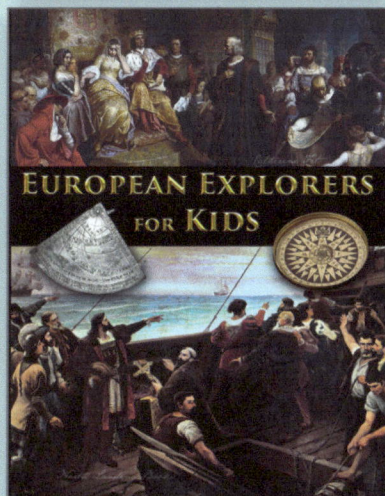
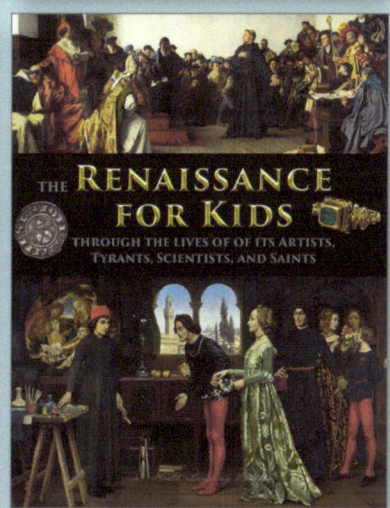
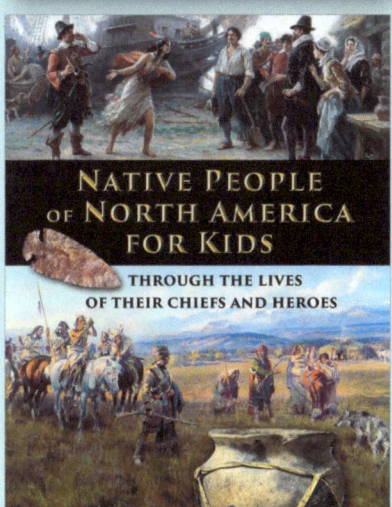
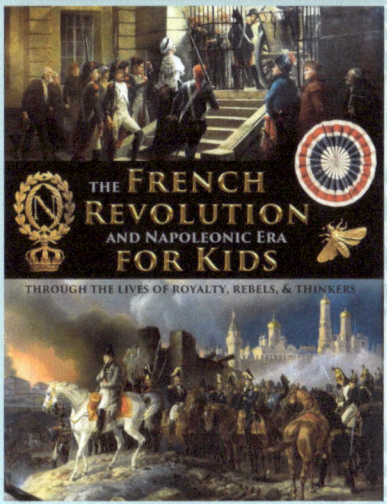
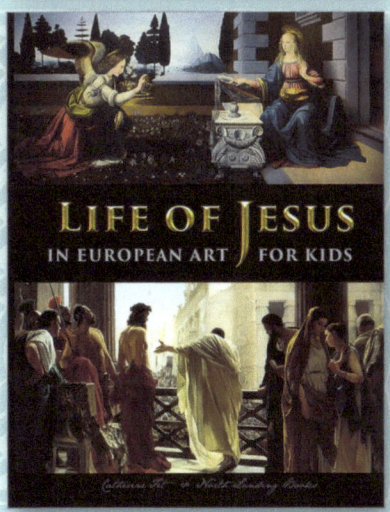

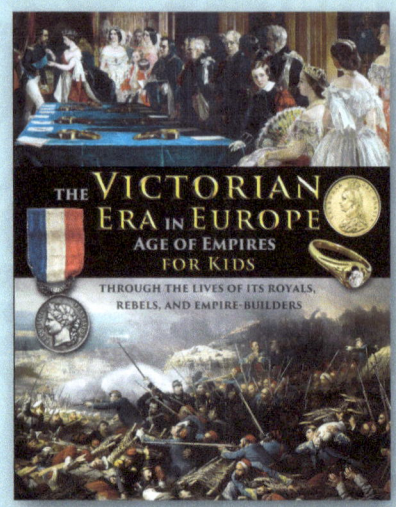
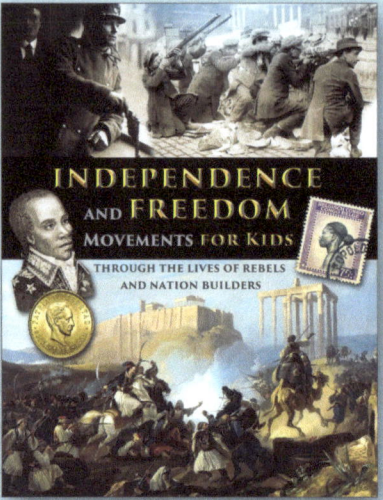

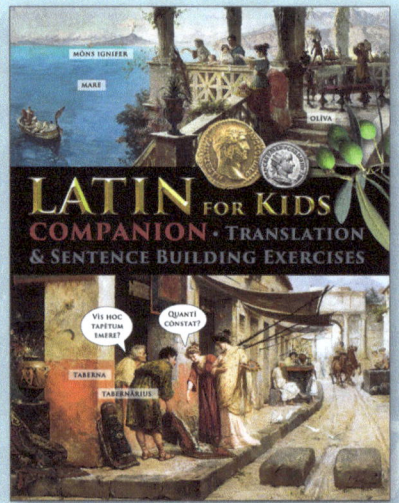

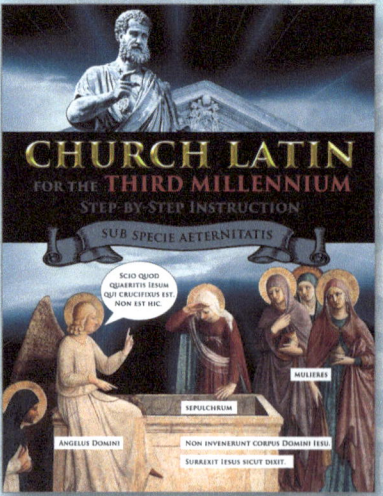

www.ingramcontent.com/pod-product-compliance
Lightning Source LLC
LaVergne TN
LVHW070438070526
838199LV00036B/663